THE VANCOUVER CANUCKS

The Best Players and the Greatest Games

Stephen Drake

OVER TIME BOOKS

The Publisher: OverTime Books is an imprint of Éditions de la Montagne Verte

Library and Archives Canada Cataloguing in Publication

Drake, Stephen, 1960–
    The Vancouver Canucks / Stephen Drake.

Includes bibliographical references.
ISBN 13: 978-1-897277-24-9
ISBN 10: 1-897277-24-5

    1. Vancouver Canucks (Hockey team)—History. I. Title.

GV848.V35D73 2007   796.962'640971133   C2007-904332-1

Project Director: J. Alexander Poulton
Production: Alexander Luthor
Proofreader: Jordan Allan
Cover Image: CP/photo by Mark Avery

PC: P5

Dedication

To my wife Julia, for bringing me coffee on
Saturday mornings, and to my daughter
Emily and my son Benjamin, whose sweet
voices drifted down to the basement as I
tapped away on this book.

Acknowledgements

The Vancouver Canucks have never reached the ultimate goal of winning a Stanley Cup, but the city has produced a number of first-rate authors, sportswriters and broadcasters who have chronicled the team's bumpy history. Part of the pleasure in writing this book was reading the work of Denny Boyd, Archie McDonald, Tony Gallagher, Kerry Banks, Ian McIntyre and the many other beat writers and newspaper columnists who have so vividly recorded the team's journey. Vancouver has also been blessed to have the voices of Jim Robson, Jim Hughson and John Shorthouse bring the games to us at home, at work and on the road. Their passion for the game has helped keep me a fan for all these years.

Contents

Introduction

December 1982.

The Montréal Canadiens are in town, and the Pacific Coliseum is sold out. The atmosphere inside the rink on Renfrew Street is always electric when the Habs visit. The powerhouse Canadiens, the most successful team in NHL history, have devoted fans in every part of the country.

As the game unfolds, the drama centers around Vancouver right winger Stan Smyl and his left winger counterpart on Montréal, the great defensive specialist Bob Gainey. Both players are among the best body checkers in hockey, and for the next 60 minutes, they pound each either with one devastating hit after another.

It is survival of the fittest, with neither player able to gain an advantage over the other. The great Montréal sportswriter Red Fisher, who had seen many hockey wars, declared afterward, "I've never seen anything like that."

For the last 36 years, the Vancouver Canucks have been trying to win their first Stanley Cup. It took the team 12 years from its expansion inception in 1970 to win its first playoff series. Canucks fans suffered through 19 losing seasons in the team's first 21 years of existence.

And through those dismal decades, there was no resident superstar to provide some heroic interludes. Vancouver supporters had to be content with the performances of foot soldiers like Smyl, who doggedly battled against the hockey powers that drifted into town. The rink would be full to watch Bobby Orr, Guy Lafleur and Wayne Gretzky weave their magic, with the local fans left wondering why they couldn't get one of those.

From Greg Adams to Peter Zezel, over 400 players have worn the Vancouver jersey. It took over two decades and the arrival of Pavel Bure for a Canuck to win a league trophy or be named a First or Second Team All-Star. The most popular Vancouver players in the early years were all second-tier talents who played hard and enjoyed some success—flaky Gary Smith, who would give his coaches heartburn by stickhandling up the ice, hoping to become the first NHL netminder to score a goal; the lumbering Harold Snepsts, who every once in a while would try going end-to-end like the great Orr; and the human fire hydrant Smyl, who would recklessly throw his five-foot-eight-inch frame into the biggest targets he could find.

In 1982, a gift came from the hockey gods—an improbable run to a Stanley Cup final. For eight weeks, the city embraced a rag-tag group of overachieving hockey warriors. Towel power was born. The unexpected journey ended in four straight losses to the powerful New York Islanders. The result couldn't be judged a letdown; Vancouver had vanquished three equally mediocre teams before being overmatched in the final series.

For the next 12 years, there would be another long drought of playoff success. In 1991, Bure arrived in Vancouver. The Russian Rocket, the team's first superstar, was the only ingredient missing in a talented lineup that Pat Quinn had put together. Two straight playoff setbacks followed before another appearance in the 1994 Stanley Cup final.

Over seven wonderful games, Vancouver battled the New York Rangers. In game seven, the Canucks ended up one goalpost short of sending the outcome to overtime. It was an agonizing way to lose a Cup. Sixty thousand disgruntled supporters descended on the downtown core after the game. A combination of alcohol and frustration provided the recipe for violence. The ensuing riot resulted in more than $1 million in damage.

Then came more rebuilding and success through the Brian Burke years. Markus Naslund and Todd Bertuzzi became the most feared offensive duo in hockey, but the Canucks never adapted their game for a playoff run. Twice they blew 3–1 series leads, in both cases losing the deciding game on home ice. The team imploded for good when Bertuzzi attacked Steve Moore in 2004 and Burke was made accountable for the lack of post-season victories.

Over the last 36 years, through all the highs and lows, Vancouver has remained a hockey town. The enthusiasm for the game hasn't diminished since the days of Orland Kurtenbach and Andre Boudrias. For 168 games, a span of four years, GM Place has been full every night, with 18,630 fans showing up at the downtown rink. Canucks news dominates the sports media in the city.

General manager Dave Nonis has made 27-year-old goaltender Roberto Luongo the centerpiece of the current Canucks roster. Over the

coming years, the team's first superstar goaltender will be asked to lead the team to the 16 playoff victories required to bring a Cup to the West
Coast.

Winning the Stanley Cup is more difficult
than ever—30 teams set the same goal. The salary cap era has brought parity—hockey outposts
like Tampa Bay and Carolina have won the trophy in recent years. Vancouver fans are patiently
waiting their turn.

Chapter One

How Hockey Arrived on the West Coast

In a much earlier time...before Roberto Luongo, Markus Naslund, Pavel Bure, Trevor Linden, Richard Brodeur, Stan Smyl or Orland Kurtenbach ever put on a uniform, Vancouver fans had the most exciting hockey player in the world in their own backyard. Before GM Place or the Pacific Coliseum was built, Vancouver had a hockey palace that was among the best in the world. And before Dave Nonis, Brian Burke, Pat Quinn or Harry Neale came to town, two brothers from eastern Canada had a vision to bring hockey to the West Coast. Indeed, Vancouver has a long history of professional hockey that goes back almost to the sport's earliest roots. To be precise, hockey arrived on January 5, 1912.

Vancouver was a thriving community of just over 100,000. It was a boom time; the city was hailed as Canada's Gateway to the Orient. The docks never slept. Land prices spiraled upward;

a new six-room bungalow in the popular Kitsilano area listed for $4800.

Where there's money, there's opportunity. The Patrick family had come west from Quebec in 1907, quickly amassing a lumbering fortune in the Kootenays. Eldest sons Lester and Frank helped their father establish the Patrick Lumber Company, but their hearts were still in the East, where both had excelled at sports. They were especially talented at hockey, and both brothers divided their time between British Columbia, Québec and Ontario to continue playing.

The popularity of the sport in the eastern part of Canada and the gold rush economy of British Columbia convinced the Patrick boys that the sport could become a moneymaker on the West Coast. The temperate climate meant artificial ice-rinks would have to be constructed—an expensive proposition in a time when only eight such facilities existed in the world.

It would have been fun to eavesdrop on Lester and Frank as they somehow convinced their father to sell off his timber holdings to fund a new hockey league. Almost $400,000 came out of the family's fortune to build two rinks: one in Vancouver, the other in Victoria. The Vancouver rink, a wood and brick structure, was completed in less than a year and was the largest. Built on

Denman Street in the city's West End, "the Pile," as it became affectionately known by the city's citizens, towered over the shipyard on Coal Harbour. The arena could seat 10,500 people, fully 10 percent of the area's population. Only the Madison Square Garden complex in New York was larger. The Patrick brothers were convinced fans would come out to watch a sport most people had never seen before.

The brothers were opposites in temperament. Frank was the quieter brother, but his keen mind was well respected in hockey circles. In 1933, he was named the managing director of the NHL, a title that included overseeing the officials and making rulings on suspensions. Lester was outgoing and always the life of the party. He would become a legend in New York, when, as the coach of the Rangers in 1928, he came off the bench at the age of 44 (his nickname by this time was the "Silver Fox" because of his full head of gray hair) to tend goal in the Stanley Cup final against the Montréal Maroons. Lester was an emergency replacement when the regular goalie was hurt (in those days some teams had only one netminder). He stopped all 16 shots he faced—the Rangers won the game in overtime and went on to win the Cup. Together, the two brothers had grand dreams for the sport to succeed in British Columbia.

As the first game drew nearer, there was a growing excitement within the community. The Patrick brothers wooed established stars from the eastern league. The newspapers in Ottawa and Montréal wrote scathing editorials on the disloyalty of the brothers in betraying their ex-teams, but that didn't stop them from signing top players such as scoring sensation Newsy Lalonde. The new Pacific Coast Hockey Association (PCHA) was to consist of three teams in 1912: the Victoria Senators, the New Westminster Royals and the Vancouver Millionaires. The Royals and Million-aires would share the Denman Arena; the Senators were housed in the new Victoria rink that seated 4000 spectators. The league would run three months, with each team playing 16 games.

Five thousand fans, paying between 50 cents and two dollars, showed up to see the Million-aires defeat the Royals 8–3 in the league opener. The Millionaires colors were maroon and white; dark red, wool sweaters had white collars and cuffs and a white "V" down the front with matching maroon stockings. The crowd, at first hushed, watching a sport they had never seen before, soon began to cheer wildly as the puck flashed around the ice.

The crowds were consistent, but not spectacu-lar, for the rest of the season; the Patricks were unable to fill the Denman rink. The year was salvaged when the brothers proposed an All-Star challenge against the best players in the East. The three-game series was a huge success, as over 8000 fans showed up for one of the games. The star attraction was Fred "Cyclone" Taylor, who was the most exciting player of his time.

The next season, the Patricks lured Taylor to the West Coast with hockey's biggest salary, $1800 per season. It turned out to be a bargain. Taylor's sensational skating and accurate shooting drew 7400 fans to the first game. For the next contest, a crowd of 10,500 showed up—the largest crowd to ever see a hockey game anywhere in the world. Taylor was the key. A small but tough forward, he had dazzled crowds in professional hockey towns in the East for five seasons. His skating speed had earned him the nicknames "Tornado" and "Whirlwind," but when a Montréal reporter overheard the Governor General of the day describe him as "a cyclone if I ever saw one," the new name stuck for good.

After convincing Taylor to settle down in Vancouver, the sport continued to grow. The Patricks fought to have a western challenge to the Stanley Cup, and in 1915, the Millionaires hosted the championship. Led by Taylor's seven goals, Vancouver swept the Ottawa Senators in three straight games. Frank Patrick, the Vancouver general manager and coach, had assembled one of hockey's greatest teams; all seven starters—they had one extra player on the ice back then called the "rover"—were inducted into the Hockey Hall of Fame. It was fitting that the sport's biggest palace hosted the coronation of the new kings of hockey.

The Patrick brothers constantly tinkered with the game, leaving a legacy as two of hockey's all-time innovators. They placed numbers on the players' jerseys for easy identification, allowed goalies to fall down and wander from the net, and instituted the penalty shot and the recording of assists. They painted blue lines on the ice to set up the off-side rule and allowed players to kick the puck. They standardized the nights for home games and brought in the double referee system. Perhaps most significantly, the Patricks were the first to devise a playoff system for their league—a concept now used in every other professional team sport in North America.

The Patricks also expanded hockey south of the border. In the 1914–15 season, the New Westminster team relocated to Portland, and a year later, Seattle joined the league. The Seattle Metropolitans built a powerhouse team and, in 1917, became the first American squad to win a Stanley Cup. These were the glory years for the PCHA. Vancouver made another challenge for the Stanley Cup in 1918, but this time lost to the Toronto Arenas.

Times change, however, and by the time Taylor retired in 1921, the NHL clubs had begun to lure top players back east. In 1925, the PCHA merged with the Western Canada Hockey League, but a year later, the Patricks knew it was all over and sold their players to the NHL for $300,000. The family did keep their arenas, and in 1927, 11,000 people filled the Denman rink to watch the Toronto Grads defeat the Fort William Thundering Herd to win the Allan Cup as Canadian amateur champions.

Their hockey empire collapsed nine years later when, at about 3:00AM on August 20, 1936, one of the loudest and most terrifying sounds in the 50-year history of Vancouver woke up residents all over the city. A fire had raced through the arena, and the roof had come crashing down. It was a four-alarm blaze, bringing out every available fireman in the city. It was a grand final performance. "The fire jumped up the rows of seats inside the arena like a man walking up stairs," said J.A. Thomas, the fire marshall at the time.

Fortunately the wind was calm that night, otherwise the whole West End might have gone up in flames. Three firemen were hurt in their two-hour battle against the fire, but no lives were lost. No cause for the blaze was ever determined. An estimated 20,000 people crowded into the neighborhood to watch the rink burn. Among them was Cyclone Taylor.

The destruction of the Denman Arena was a huge loss to the city. The seating capacity of the building attracted top athletes from other sports. Boxing legends Jack Dempsey and Jack Johnson came to town, as did tennis superstar Suzanne Lenglen. There were huge political gatherings to hear prime ministers Mackenzie King and R.B. Bennett. And entertainers from around the world stopped in Vancouver: piano virtuosos, top opera stars and popular crooners. There were marathon dances, six-day cycle events and entertainment extravaganzas of all types to help people weather the Depression of the 1930s. "When you look back you realize the Arena, though just a square building, nothing to look at, was a pleasant sport spot. It evolved that anything big naturally went down Denman Street way. Generally you felt before you started it was going to be worthwhile just because it was there," reported Hal Straight in the *Vancouver Sun* after the rink burned down.

The Patricks had established the foundation for hockey to remain as one of Vancouver's passions. Even though the sport would not have such a grand home for another 30 years, hockey stayed in the city. In the 1930s and '40s, semi-pro teams competed for the Allan Cup, and amateur hockey remained popular. In 1948, the Pacific Coast League (PCL) was formed and included teams in Vancouver, New Westminster and Victoria. Future NHL players like Gump Worsley, Johnny Bower, Cesare Maniago, Tony Esposito, Andy Bathgate, Allan Stanley and Lou Fontinato played in the Lower Mainland.

The PCL evolved into the Western Hockey League (WHL), which included teams in the United States. Over the next 20 years, the Vancouver franchise, called the Canucks, often played to packed houses in the 5080-seat PNE Forum and won four championships. In 1966, the team was sold to a group of local businessmen who were laying the groundwork for Vancouver to be admitted to the NHL to fight for the Stanley Cup once again.

Chapter Two

Black Tuesday as the NHL Comes to Town

In 1965, the NHL announced that it would double its size from six to 12 teams in time for the 1967–68 season. Vancouver was ready—all three levels of government had contributed funding to construct a $6 million circular arena on the PNE grounds that could hold just over 16,000 fans. The Pacific Coliseum, as it was later called, was the hockey facility the city had lacked to bring the big league to town earlier.

To the shock of Vancouver sports fans, the NHL turned down a bid by a local group led by Cyrus H. McLean. The governors had been lobbied by another Vancouver-based group led by oil-magnate and millionaire sportsman Frank McMahon. The league ordered the rival groups to merge their resources. In return, Vancouver was promised first consideration when the NHL next expanded.

In 1969, the league announced it would add two more teams in time for the 1970–71 season, and Vancouver would be one of the franchises if it could raise the $6 million expansion fee. It was a huge sum for the time and forced the group to look outside Canada for the money. In 1970, a company from Minnesota called Medicor (Medical Investment Corporation) bought majority interest in the team, and the Vancouver Canucks, along with the Buffalo Sabres, were formally accepted into the NHL. The first general manager of the team was Hall of Famer Norman "Bud" Poile, who three years earlier had put together the Philadelphia Flyers expansion team. Hal Laycoe, who the year before lasted only 24 games as the Los Angeles Kings coach, was named the Canucks head coach. Next came getting some players.

For $6 million, Vancouver and Buffalo would first get to take turns drafting 20 unprotected players (18 skaters and two goalies) from the other 12 NHL teams; then both teams would get first crack at the best junior players in the amateur draft. Vancouver lost the spin of the roulette wheel on the expansion draft, but managed to pick some solid players in goalies Dunc Wilson and Charlie Hodge, defencemen Gary Doak and Pat Quinn, and forwards Orland Kurtenbach and Rosaire Paiement. The amateur draft held the greater prize. The first-pick winner would get the right to select Gilbert Perreault, a superstar in the making, from the two-time Memorial Cup champion Montréal Junior Canadiens. Perreault's rink-long dashes in the junior ranks brought fans to their feet. Hockey experts agreed that the big, fast-skating forward could be a franchise-maker.

On June 9, 1970, in front of a large audience in the Grand Salon of the Queen Elizabeth Hotel in Montréal, NHL president Clarence Campbell spun a large roulette wheel to decide who would pick first. Poile went with the even numbers for the Canucks; Buffalo genaral manager Punch Imlach was left with odds. When Campbell spun the wheel, the crowd went silent. When it finally stopped, the Campbell yelled, "Number two! Vancouver wins first choice in the amateur draft."

The Canucks contingent went crazy, but the celebration was short-lived. Imlach was on his feet, as was everyone on the Buffalo side, yelling, "Eleven, eleven!" A confused Campbell looked again and embarrassingly announced, "There has been a mistake. The winning number is eleven." The Vancouver supporters went quiet.

In Imlach's book, *Heaven and Hell in the NHL*, the crusty general manager and coach explained the significance of the spin going Buffalo's way:

"I wore my knees out praying that I would win first choice in the amateur draft. I wanted Gilbert Perreault as I had never wanted a hockey player before. I'd seen him play that spring and the hair just stood up on my neck at what he could do. He was a superstar in the making, the man the Buffalo franchise could be built around."

The Stanley Cup-winning executive's instincts were right. Perreault won the Calder Trophy as Rookie of the Year and went on to play his entire 17-year career for the Sabres. Out of a bow-legged stance, the young forward amazed Buffalo fans with his fast skating and endless repertoire of fakes and moves. With Perreault, the Sabres became a model expansion franchise, quickly moving up the standings to make the Stanley Cup final in 1975. As the years passed by, Vancouver sportswriters referred to that day in Montréal as "Black Tuesday."

Vancouver has been incredibly unlucky with their top selections at the draft table each June. Over the years, the team's list of first-round choices has produced some solid NHL players, but never a dynamo who would bring fans to the rink. Dale Tallon was the first on the list. Tallon was a talented, mobile player, capable of playing either forward or defence. He also had good looks and an impressive sporting resume that included a Canadian Amateur Golf Championship. He showed up for his first press conference as a Canuck in a wildly colorful outfit that was the fashion style of the early 1970s and was promptly nicknamed "Englebert" in honor of the showy lounge singer. Despite posting some impressive offensive numbers, the Canucks were never able to decide if Tallon should play up front or stay on the blue line. After three frustrating seasons, he demanded to be traded. The Canucks obliged, sending him to Chicago, where he completed his playing days before retiring in 1980.

The list of first-round frustration is a sore spot for many Canucks fans. Along with Tallon, Jocelyn Guevremont, Don Lever, Dennis Ververgaert, Rick Blight, Jere Gillis, Bill Derlago, Rick Vaive, Rick Lanz and Garth Butcher were the team's selections in the first dozen years. Some of the names on the list ended up having many solid years in a Canucks uniform (Lever and Butcher); some had their best years on other teams (Guevremont and Vaive); others were shooting stars that lit up the league for a few moments before quickly fading away. None of them ended up becoming Hall of Fame candidates.

Still, as the Canucks prepared to open their first season, there was great anticipation and enthusiasm in the city as big league hockey returned to the West Coast. Fans were ready to cheer for a 20-player roster full of cast-offs from the league's other teams. The lineup that would start the year in the blue, white and green uniforms with the stick-in-the-rink crest had a grand total of 37 NHL goals between them in the previous season.

Vancouver's first roster was a hard-working, tough group led by Kurtenbach. At age 34, the first Canucks captain had battled back injuries through much of his career and, in 1968, had endured a spinal fusion operation while with the New York Rangers. Yet when Kurtenbach was healthy, the tall, rangy forward had a Jean Beliveau-like grace as he moved around the ice. Opponents gave him lots of space, too, because Kurtenbach had such a feared reputation as a fighter that he was rarely challenged. Like most of the first-year Canucks, Kurtenbach wanted to be in Vancouver. He had fond memories of the city, winning Rookie of the Year honors in 1958 as a member of the WHL Canucks. Kurtenbach, much like the other members of the team, was looking for the opportunity to play a bigger role and reach his true potential as an NHL player.

On October 9, 1970, the Vancouver Canucks made their debut against the Los Angeles Kings in a game televised throughout the country on

Hockey Night in Canada. In front of a packed house at the Coliseum, which included political dignitaries from all levels of government, the Los Angeles Kings mowed the Canucks down 3–1. The pre-game ceremony was highlighted by a display of the Stanley Cup at center ice and by a special appearance by Cyclone Taylor, who, at 82 years of age, was introduced as Vancouver's hockey player of the century.

The Canucks' first win came two days later when they beat the Toronto Maple Leafs 5–3 in front of the home crowd. Led by Kurtenbach's 53 points in the team's first 51 games, Vancouver battled for fourth place in the tough Eastern Division. Any playoff dreams were dashed after Christmas when a Bobby Baun bodycheck put Kurtenbach out for 27 games with a knee injury. In the end, Vancouver won 24 games to finish sixth, 26 points out of a playoff spot.

There were plenty of highlights for a first-year expansion team. Six players had 20 goals or more, led by Paiement with 34. The tough winger had also accumulated 152 minutes in penalties and twice bettered the league's best player, Bobby Orr, in fisticuffs. Perhaps the highlight of the first season was Paiement's four goals as Vancouver beat the defending Stanley Cup champion Bruins 5–4. The fans also took to a little forward who was claimed from Minnesota in the expansion draft: Andre Boudrias was nicknamed "Super-pest" in a checking role, as he was often assigned to stop the top scorers on the other team. In Vancouver, number seven blossomed as an offensive force, leading the club in scoring in four of the team's first five seasons. Vancouver received a surprising boost in goal from veteran netminder Charlie Hodge. A Stanley Cup winner with Montréal in a backup role, Hodge managed a winning record with the Canucks (15-13-5). And, though over-shadowed by Perreault in Buffalo, Tallon contributed a solid 42 points in his rookie season on the blue line.

Most importantly, the Canucks were a hit with the Vancouver sporting public. In the expansion year, the rink was filled to 97.5 percent of total capacity as almost 654,000 fans made the trip to Renfrew Street. The team had a waiting list of 3000 people who wanted season tickets. During a March game against Detroit at the Coliseum, 700 fans came out to watch a closed circuit television broadcast in the Agrodome next door. Vancouver had proved it was now a big league hockey town.

Chapter Three

The Long Road to Respectability

For the next six years, change was the only constant. At the end of the team's second season, general manager Bud Poile was forced to resign because of health concerns. Coach Hal Laycoe stepped in as the acting general manager and hired Vic Stasiuk to coach. Boudrias and Kurtenbach were the only consistent offensive forces in that second year, sharing the team's scoring lead with 61 points each as the Canucks lost 50 games and fell to seventh spot. Paiement's production dropped to 10 goals—the winger even hired the renowned hypnotist Reveen to end his goal drought and then went 17 games without scoring. First-round pick Jocelyn Guevremont, a big defenceman out of Québec junior hockey, finished third in scoring with 13 goals and 38 assists.

Starting season three, the Canucks added first-round pick Don Lever to the lineup. The forward from Niagara Falls would play the next eight seasons in Vancouver. The team finished well out of the playoffs again. Boudrias had 30 goals and 40 assists, but it was the emergence of Bobby Schmautz as a complete NHL player that excited the fans. "Schmautzie" had proved his toughness when he was first called up from the minors, but no one expected the 38 goals and 33 assists he added in his first full season.

In the off-season, the team made its first major trade as the unhappy Tallon was sent to the Chicago Black Hawks in return for goaltender Gary Smith and defenceman Jerry Korab. Stasiuk was fired and replaced by new coach Bill McCreary.

Heading into their fourth season, the Canucks were no longer the only game in town. The rival World Hockey Association entered the Vancouver market when a group of businessmen led by Jimmy Pattison brought the Philadelphia franchise to the Pacific Coliseum. The new Vancouver Blazers received 5000 ticket applications in their first three weeks. Fortunately, the Blazers were just as bad as the Canucks on the ice, but they still averaged over 9300 fans in their first season.

The Canucks opened the 1973–74 campaign by playing better than .500 hockey in their first 10 games, but winning only one contest in their next 19 spelled the end for McCreary. In January 1974, McCreary was fired and replaced by Phil Maloney. A former star with the WHL Canucks and known as the "Silver Fox" for his thick thatch of white hair, Maloney had been coaching the Canucks' farm team in Seattle before taking over the big club. Seventeen days after taking over the coaching job, Maloney was also named general manager. A shy man by nature, Maloney admitted that if coaching hadn't panned out, he'd have been quite comfortable running a fishing or hunting camp in the wilderness.

The new boss brought a refreshing approach to a languishing franchise. For the remaining 37 games, Maloney concentrated on bringing a new attitude to the team. "I'd like to instill some pride in these people if it's possible. You know, you can't fool the people in the stands. They will go along with you only as long as they know you are giving it everything you've got."

The Canucks ended the 1973–74 season with 59 points. Even though the team finished 17 points out of a playoff spot, Maloney believed the Canucks had turned a corner. The acquisition of Smith had solidified the goaltending position. Lever was emerging as a solid NHL player, with 23 goals. Rookie Dennis Ververgaert started slowly, but the first-round selection finished with

26 goals and 31 assists. The ever-dependable Boudrias set a team record with 75 points. Maloney made one trade before the season ended, sending the popular Schmautz to Boston for Chris Oddleifson, a young center who would provide some scoring depth.

Over the summer, the team was sold to local media baron Frank Griffiths, the owner of the Western Broadcasting Company, for $9 million. The club's original owner, Tom Scallen, a Minneapolis-based businessman, was forced to sell the Canucks when he was charged with fraud that involved the funneling of team funds into other businesses. Scallen, the head of Medicor, was later found guilty of stealing $3 million in club funds to keep the rest of his empire afloat.

"We bought the hockey shares when we were away in the Caribbean," recalled Griffiths several years later when asked about the circumstances surrounding the sale of the team. "The previous owner had gone to jail, and the team was available for what seemed a fair price. We had done very well in the broadcasting business and were prepared to put something back into the community."

Griffiths was a charted accountant by profession. He kept a low profile in his role as owner of the team. Through the coming years, players would come and go and there would be coaching changes and upheavals in the ranks of upper management. The one constant was ownership—Griffiths could be criticized for some of the general managers that he hired, but through the bad years, the owner never wavered in his commitment to the team.

There was big-time pressure for the Canucks to gain a playoff spot in the 1974–75 season. The rival Vancouver Blazers had hired popular coach Joe Crozier—the former bench boss of the WHL Canucks—to take over the team, and Canucks season ticket sales had begun to decline. Further expansion in the NHL had meant a realignment of the league. Vancouver was moved out of the tough Eastern Division and into the five-team Smythe Division with St. Louis, Chicago, Minnesota and Kansas City. In future years, the group would be known as the "Sweathog Division," in reference to the lack of quality teams. Even with the realignment, the Canucks would need everything to go their way to make the playoffs. A fast start would make it easier, and the team responded with a 22-10-5 record through December.

During the first half of the season, it became clear that Gary Smith could become Vancouver's first Hart Trophy candidate as the league's Most Valuable Player. Smith came to the Canucks with the reputation as one in a long line of flaky goalies. In his first press conference after the trade to Vancouver, he lived up to the billing when he declared, "Yes, everything you've heard about me is absolutely true...I am a tremendous goalie."

Tall and lanky in the Ken Dryden mold, the frizzy-haired Smith came to the Canucks with some solid credentials after sharing the Vezina Trophy with Tony Esposito in Chicago. He was six feet, four inches tall and 215 pounds, so he covered a lot of the net even when he wasn't moving. Smith was the zaniest of all Canucks goalies. He took off all his equipment between periods and put it back on again. He wanted to be the first goaltender to score an NHL goal and would often stickhandle around opposing players, sometimes coming out past his blue line. His other ambition was to punt the puck over the scoreboard in Maple Leaf Gardens; he once managed to clear his zone that way. He hated to practice. One of his favorite moves during the game was to lift the net off its moorings in pressure situations to get a faceoff.

Early in the season, Maloney knew he had a special goalie. In October, the Canucks went into Madison Square Garden and shut out the New York Rangers 1–0. After the game, the Canucks general manager and coach said it was the most fantastic display of goaltending he had ever seen. Flyers coach Fred Shero called the Canucks a "one-man team" in reference to Smith's acrobatics.

As the year progressed, Smith became the team's leader on the ice and the organizer of social functions away from the rink. "The players followed Smitty like a pied piper," recalled Maloney in a 1990 interview with Grant Kerr from the *Vancouver Province* newspaper. "He'd walk into an airport in wooden shoes, no socks and a fur coat down to his ankles. He'd kick his shoes in the air and there'd be 20 guys running after them, yelling, 'I got it!' We had camaraderie, good togetherness."

Maloney used his greatest asset as much as possible. Smith played in 72 games and finished with a 32-24-9 record, a 3.09 goals-against average and six shutouts. They were all team records for a Canucks starting goalie. At the end of the season, Smith came in fifth in voting for the Hart Trophy, the highest of any Vancouver player until Pavel Bure came along almost 20 years later.

Smith wasn't the only Canuck to have a career season. Vancouver was eighth in league scoring. For the first time, they had a true "big line" made up of Boudrias, who set another team scoring record with 78 points, Lever, who had 68 points, and Ververgaert, who had 51 points in only 57 games. They weren't just a one-line team, however; nine forwards had 16 or more goals.

Maloney revamped the defence corps. The mostly gentle giant Bob Dailey had 48 points. Dennis Kearns was the slick passer who set up the power play. Tracy Pratt and Mike Robitaille teamed together to play against the other teams' stars. John Grisdale and a mid-season call-up named Harold Snepsts rounded out the top six.

On New Year's Day, the Canucks' season began to stall. It started with a 2–0 home loss to the Philadelphia Flyers, then six straight road losses, followed by another two defeats at the Pacific Coliseum. Despite the team record nine-game losing streak, Vancouver rebounded to go 16-13-5 the rest of the way. Not only had the Canucks qualified for the playoffs, they won first place in the Smythe Division with 38 wins, 32 losses and 10 ties.

Vancouver's reward for a division title was a first-round bye, but in the second round, they were matched up against the Montréal Canadiens, a team that finished tied with Buffalo and Philadelphia with the league's best record. The Habs had a deep roster full of Hall of Fame candidates. Guy Lafleur had finished fourth in league scoring with 119 points, and line-mate Peter Mahovlich was fifth with 117. On defence, the Canucks had to contend with Guy Lapointe and Serge Savard. And then there was Ken Dryden in goal. Worst of all, Vancouver had never beaten Montréal in 26 regular season games over five years.

Maloney played a hunch in game one at the Forum, starting goalie Ken Lockett instead of Smith, who had missed the last two weeks of the season with an injury. The backup netminder entered the playoffs on a mini hot streak, having notched two straight shutouts in the final days of the season. The move didn't work out as Montréal dominated in a 6–2 victory. Smith was back in net for game two. Rested and confident, the lanky netminder made 38 saves to steal a 2–1 victory in hostile territory to notch the team's first post-season win.

Back in Vancouver for game three, long-deprived Canucks fans were eagerly anticipating the team's first playoff game on home ice. The home crowd welcomed their heroes with a deafening roar, and the rink got even louder when John Gould scored three minutes into the opening period. The Canadiens were too good a team to get flustered, storming back to score four straight goals for a 4–1 victory. Two nights later, the Habs again turned aside the home team with a 4–0 win.

Game five was back in Montréal, and the Canucks pushed the Canadiens into overtime. At 17:06 of the first overtime, Lafleur won the series when he threw the puck out of the corner to the front of the net. Before Smith could handle the puck, Kearns tried to knock it out of the air. Instead, the puck hit his stick at a funny angle and went by Smith into the Canucks net. The Vancouver goalie skated right off the ice and went straight into the dressing room. The magical ride was over, but the Canucks' success rejuvenated the team and the fans. Jimmy Pattison, sensing his Blazers would fade totally out the city's consciousness, moved his team to Calgary in the off-season.

Trying to stay on top after a Cinderella season is always tough, but Maloney hoped the addition of 10th pick Rick Blight from the WHL's Brandon Wheat Kings would give the team another weapon. The forward came through with 25 goals and 31 assists. Unlike the 1974–75 campaign, the Canucks started the season slowly, only managing to reach the .500 mark by early January. Smith wasn't able to steal as many games, and despite another year of balanced scoring led by Ververgaert (71 points), Lever (65 points) and Oddleifson (62 points), the team was never able to recapture the magic of the year before. Still, Maloney guided the team to a second straight playoff berth, this time finishing second in the Smythe Division.

With no bye in the first round of the playoffs, Vancouver would have to face the New York Islanders, a team that had improved for four straight years, skyrocketing to 101 points during the regular season. Led by rookie Bryan Trottier and defenceman Denis Potvin, the Islanders swept the Canucks in the best of three series, winning the opener 5–3 in Long Island and the second game 3–1 in Vancouver.

It had been a disappointing season, and Maloney felt the team slipping back to its pre-playoff form. During the summer, he concentrated on his duties as general manager. Smith, the cornerstone of the team, was traded after only three seasons to Minnesota for goalie Cesare Maniago. Boudrias, the team's all-time leading scorer, had retired, but with the addition of Mike "Shaky" Walton, Maloney hoped to replace any lost offence.

The team struggled in the opening months of the 1976–77 season and by Christmas had only nine wins in 35 games. Maloney removed himself from the bench and appointed Orland Kurtenbach as the head coach. Captain Kurt had guided the Tulsa Oilers to a Central Hockey League championship the year before, but not even a 10-game undefeated streak at the end of the season could get the team back in the playoffs. In May 1977, Maloney was dismissed as general manger, and veteran NHL executive Jake Milford was brought in to run the team. It was time to rebuild again.

Chapter Four

Haar-old, the Steamer and Tiger

Jake Milford came into Vancouver with 40
years experience as a player, scout, coach,
manager and administrator. Frank Griffiths
snapped him up as the new boss of hockey operations just four days after he left the general
manager post in Los Angeles. The white-haired
Milford had to have the patience of a grandfa-
ther in his first days with the team. The Canucks
had no direction, relying on a mix of discon-
tented veterans, raw rookies and fringe players.
Milford decided that Kurtenbach would be kept
as coach. With yet another high draft selection,
he chose forward Jere Gillis fourth overall. The
Canucks were competitive through the first 29
games of the 1977–78 season, but finished well
out of a playoff spot with a 20-43-7 record. Gillis
performed admirably in his rookie season, scoring 23 goals.

The fan favorite in those bleak years was Harold Snepsts. A third-round draft pick in 1974, Snepsts was called up from the minors the next season to bring some much needed muscle to the blue line. His big frame (six feet, three inches tall and 215 pounds), menacing scowl, Fu Manchu moustache and helmet-less mop of thinning hair, combined with his grit and desire on each shift, endeared him to the fans and coaches alike. Snepsts improved his game each season, was named top Canucks defenceman on four occasions and was the team's representative in two All-Star games. Every once in a while, Snepsts would get the urge to rush the puck; as he began to build up steam, the fans would start serenading, "HAAR-OLD, HAAR-OLD, HAAR-OLD." He ended up playing 781 games in Canucks colors.

Milford had seen enough losing. The overhaul started with the dismissal of Kurtenbach after the season ended and the appointment of Harry Neale as the head coach. At 41, Neale was new to the NHL, but had built a successful track record as a coach in junior hockey, American college hockey and six seasons in the WHA with Minnesota and New England. His teams had never missed the post-season. Neale's signing came with more fanfare than any other Canucks coach. An elaborate press conference was held at the Bayshore Inn overlooking Coal Harbour and

Stanley Park. Milford hoped to send the message that the team had hired a top-tier coach to bring a winning approach.

Neale was an innovator. He hired technical-minded assistants such as Tom Watt, Roger Neilson and Ron Smith and left them alone to teach. He was a proponent of fitness and was one of the first coaches to insist his players follow a conditioning program in the off-season. Neale would allow players to run practices. At the end of the year he would award a trophy to the player who had run the best practice, and that player would get a night on the town at Neale's expense.

Over the years, the media often looked to Neale for a caustic one-liner to add some life to their stories, especially after another dreary Vancouver performance. When asked by the Canucks PR department if he could send four players to take part in a white-water raft race, he replied, "They can go if I get to pick the players." After a Toronto goaltender had an especially good game against Vancouver, he said, "Our reports say that if you're in close, shoot high and keep it away from his glove hand. So we shot it into his glove all night; we didn't believe our own reports." Another one against the Leafs, this time after Toronto scored a goal on a weird bounce, was, "We've complained to the PNE about the boards, but anything you can't fix with a forklift, you can forget."

Besides hiring Neale, Milford also made his mark at the amateur draft in 1978. Center Bill Derlago, left wing Curt Fraser and right wing Stan Smyl were selected in the first three rounds, and all of them cracked the roster to begin the new season. Some scouts saw Smyl as too small and slow to make it in the NHL, but Neale was impressed with the stocky winger's fearlessness in training camp. "The Steamer," as Smyl became known, was a winner too, having led the New Westminster Bruins to a Memorial Cup championship.

The rebuilding didn't stop there. Following the lead of teams such as Toronto, who had grabbed Borje Salming and Inge Hammerstrom from Sweden, the Canucks brought three imports to camp. Two of the new Swedes made a lasting impact. Thomas Gradin looked slight, but quickly showed he was the team's best skater and playmaker. Milford also signed stocky defenceman Lars Lindgren, who broke NHL tradition by choosing number 13.

When training camp ended, the Canucks not only had several new faces, but a new look. Gone were the traditional blue, green and white colors of the Pacific Northwest and the rather tranquil stick-in-the-rink emblem. A San Francisco-based marketing company was paid $100,000 to come up with a more aggressive theme. Yellow, black and red became the new colors. A stylized "V" replaced the crest in the front, and the new logo, a circle with a skate and the word "Canucks" forming the blade, was confined to the sleeves. The press called them "Halloween suits" and "clown outfits." When asked about the new uniforms, Neale diplomatically replied, "Well, let us say…they are at least identifiable."

In the season opener, the new coach put out an all-rookie line of Fraser-Gradin-Smyl. They each had points in an 8–2 shellacking of the Colorado Rockies and would play together all season. The three complemented each other—Gradin the smooth playmaker, Fraser with the hard shot and harder fists when challenged, and Smyl, who would run into anyone, anytime.

The Canucks improved to 63 points in 1978–79, good enough for second place in the weak Smythe Division. Ron Sedlbauer became the first 40-goal scorer in team history. Milford traded away Ververgaert at Christmas to acquire defenceman Kevin McCarthy to help on the blue line. Glen Hanlon emerged as the number one goalie of the future. In 31 games, he had a respectable 3.10 goals-against average and three shutouts.

In the first round of the playoffs, the Canucks scared the powerhouse Philadephia Flyers with a 3–2 victory in the Spectrum. With a chance to upset the Flyers at home in the best of three series, Vancouver gave up the game-winning goal and an empty netter in the last minute to lose 6–4. Back in Philadelphia for game three, the Canucks offered little resistance, losing 7–2 to end their season.

The 1979–80 season was memorable for a series of trades as Milford continued to re-make the team. In December, Sedlbauer was sent to Chicago for two utility players. Two months later, all-time leading scorer and captain Don Lever and forward Brad Smith were moved to Atlanta for forwards Darcy Rota and Ivan Boldirev. Then, just 11 days later, Bill Derlago and Rick Vaive were traded to Toronto for Dave "Tiger" Williams and Jerry Butler. The Canucks had given up on their top draft picks again (Vaive went on to score 50 goals with the Leafs), but in Williams, they had a leader who wouldn't back down from anyone. Four days after the trade, Tiger had two fights against a couple of the brawlers on Philadelphia's Broad Street Bully squad, and the Canucks served notice that no team would be able to push them around.

Smyl surprised experts around the league, leading the Canucks in goals (31), assists (47), points (78) and penalty minutes (204). The Steamer also became Vancouver's most popular player, as fans waited expectantly for each bone-crushing hit. The forward with the fire hydrant body, who *Vancouver Sun* reporter Mike Beamish called "Pete Rose on skates," Smyl made life miserable for opponents throughout his 13-year career in Vancouver. Despite never playing for a team with a .500 or better record, Smyl never let up on a check. In his eight seasons as captain, Smyl became the face of the franchise and its all-time leading scorer. His number 12 is the only retired jersey in Canucks history.

Behind the emergence of Smyl and Gradin (70 points) and the acquisitions of Williams, Rota and Boldirev, the Canucks improved to 70 points for a third place finish in the Smythe Division. They made the playoffs again but had to face their expansion cousin Buffalo Sabres, who had finished the regular season with 40 more points.

After losing the first two games on the road, Vancouver came back with a 5–4 win at home. Williams was at his agitating best. After getting involved with several players at the Sabres bench, somebody's stick clipped Buffalo coach Scotty

Bowman. The NHL Supervisor of Officials was in the press box and claimed he saw Tiger clip Bowman. Videotape failed to catch the alleged infraction, but Williams was suspended. Without their most experienced playoff performer, the Canucks lost the next game 3–1 and were eliminated from the post-season.

For the second year in a row, Milford was sharp at the draft table, selecting two defencemen, Rick Lanz and Doug Lidster, plus Swedish forward Patrick Sundstrom. All three players would have significant stays in Vancouver. The Canucks general manager also brought home original Canuck Bobby Schmautz as a free-agent signing and claimed stay-at-home defenceman Colin Campbell off waivers. And then, in a deal with the Islanders that involved the switching of fifth-round draft picks, Milford obtained a chubby goalie named Richard Brodeur. Brodeur took advantage of the new start in Vancouver. In his first game he stopped 36 of 38 shots in a 5–2 win over Philadelphia. In all, Brodeur would get into 52 games in the 1980–81 campaign to take over as the number one goalie.

Tiger Williams was the scoring star of the team that year, with 35 goals to go along with a league-leading 343 penalty minutes. Neale had developed a well-balanced attack with eight 20-goal scorers, including a surprising 27 from Schmautz. The team improved again, finishing four games below .500 with 76 points, which was good enough for another third place finish in the Smythe Division.

For the second straight season the Canucks faced Buffalo in the playoffs, and this time they were swept in three games. After 11 years in the league, Vancouver had yet to win a playoff series. The loyal fans were losing patience as season ticket sales dropped to 9000. Milford had more work to do.

Chapter Five

An Unlikely Run for the Cup

Milford looked to Europe to improve his roster. In May he signed two more Swedes, forward Lars Molin and defenceman Anders Eldebrink, to contracts. Two months later, the team made headlines in the hockey world when Milford announced the signing of two Czechs, Jiri Bubla and Ivan Hlinka.

The NHL, at that time trying to negotiate international hockey agreements with both European and Communist hockey powers, was upset with the Canucks for helping two established players defect from the Eastern Bloc. The team asked Senator Ray Perrault to use his diplomatic skills to help smooth the waters. And in hockey terms, it was a gamble to bring them over. In his prime, Bubla was one of the best defencemen in the world and Hlinka was known as a gifted offensive forward; but both were nearing the end of their careers and would have to adjust to NHL-style hockey.

On opening night the Vancouver roster included nine Europeans. Roger Neilson was the new associate coach. He had left Buffalo after being promised the Canucks head coaching position the following season. At that point, Milford would retire and Neale would become the new general manager.

The rugged Bubla fit in quickly, becoming the hardest hitter on the Canucks blue line. Hlinka struggled, and exasperated fans jeered the slim forward as he repeatedly turned circles with the puck in his own end. By Christmas, he started skating straight ahead and began to add some offensive production. However, the press reported a rift between the European and North American players. Despite Neale's denials, it was later revealed that the issue had surfaced and that the players had called a meeting to work things out.

The team struggled through Christmas, showing occasional glimpses of progress before losing to inferior teams. The Canucks were an entertaining team to watch at home (though only the most loyal fans were still showing up to the games), but a terrible team on the road. From the last day of November through to the end of February, they lost 12 in a row away from the Pacific Coliseum. On the eve of the trade deadline, Milford traded popular goalie Glen Hanlon to St. Louis for forward Jim Nill, backup goalie Rick Heinz and Tony Currie. Brodeur's fine play had made Hanlon expendable.

By mid-March, the Canucks' fortunes began to change. A 4–2 win over Montréal in the Forum ended a 27-game unbeaten streak for the Habs on home ice. Darcy Rota scored a hat-trick after Neale put him on a line with Gradin and Smyl. Brodeur made four big saves in the first period to keep Vancouver in the game.

On March 20, the team finished its visit to the province of Québec with a tilt against the Nordiques. In the third period, Tiger Williams and Peter Stastny came together near the Canucks bench. With the two combatants jostling against the glass, a Québec fan named Pierre Fournel left his fourth row seat in an attempt to grab Tiger. Neale went into the stands after Fournel and took a swing at him. Two Canuck players followed their coach, and more punches were thrown. Defenceman Kevin McCarthy stayed on the ice, but threw his glove at someone in the stands. Neilson shed his headphones and managed to calm things down before any more damage was done. The game ended in a 3–3 tie, but the incident received a lot of media attention, sending league president John Ziegler to Vancouver to hear the Canucks' side of things.

On March 27, the league suspended Neale for 10 games and Neilson took over behind the bench. It was a harsh sentence, especially in comparison to an incident earlier in the season when Philadelphia coach Paul Holmgren was suspended for only five games after hitting referee Andy van Hellemond. The incident at Le Colisée brought what had been a divided team together and became part of Canucks folklore. How much it contributed to what would come later is debatable, but after the suspension, the team went on a 6-0-3 roll and passed the Calgary Flames for second place in the division. For the first time in their history, Vancouver would get to host a playoff series.

The Canucks had improved their regular season again to 77 points, but more importantly, they were entering the playoffs on a roll. Even the news that Canucks captain McCarthy had broken his ankle during an optional practice didn't affect their composure. The team had an unbeaten coach in Neilson, and even the bookies were picking Vancouver to win the series. Jaded Canucks fans were still skeptical. A crowd of only 11,000 showed up for the first game.

Western rival Calgary would be their first-round opponent, and even though the Flames faltered through the final days of the regular season, they still had plenty of weapons in Kent Nilsson, Lanny McDonald and Jim Peplinski. On the opening shift, new captain Stan Smyl set the tone: Gradin won the faceoff at center ice and shot the puck in the Flames end; Smyl demolished a Calgary defenceman against the boards; Gradin found the loose puck and hit Smyl with a pass in front of the net; and the Steamer deposited the puck behind Flames goalie Pat Riggin. It had taken the Canucks eight seconds to take the lead. On the ensuing faceoff, Curt Fraser squared off with Flames tough guy Willie Plett. Much like Orland Kurtenbach, Fraser was too feared a fighter to have to fight much. He knocked Plett off his feet with a hard right hand, setting a tone of physical superiority that Calgary was never able to overcome. Ivan Boldirev scored a power play goal 10 minutes later, and the Canucks went on to a 5–3 win.

Calgary was better prepared for game two. They took the play to Vancouver and scored first on a Ken Houston goal. Young Marc Crawford replied for the Canucks after a nice pass from Boldirev. Brodeur kept the Flames at bay through the third period. Early in overtime, Houston set up Peplinski with a perfect pass, but the Canucks goalie kicked the puck away. At 14:20 of the first overtime, Snepsts went on one of his occasional forays into the opposing team's end. Realizing this might turn into trouble, the steady defender stopped 20 feet inside the line and hit Lars Molin with a pass. Riggin stopped Molin's shot, but the puck slid over to Williams. As he was being cross-checked to the ice, Tiger's back hand shot slid through the Flames goalie and into the net.

Back in the old and tiny Calgary Corral for the third game, Peplinski and Gradin traded power play goals. The Flames pounded the Canucks defence, but Brodeur calmly withstood the onslaught, stopping 29 of Calgary's first 30 shots. Early in the third period, Lars Lindgren went down with a shoulder injury. Doug Halward, just back from his suspension in the Québec City incident, was forced into more action than originally planned. As the third period wore on, Vancouver started to become more dangerous. Eight minutes in, Williams took a pass on a three-on-two break and slid it under Riggin. For the second straight game, the Canucks tough guy scored the winner as Gradin notched the insurance marker in the 3–1 victory. Williams had redeemed a terrible regular season with the two big goals, plus he had shut down his old Toronto teammate, Lanny McDonald, who failed to score in the series. Brodeur, however, was the difference. The chubby goalie had a goals-against average of 1.55 and stopped 103 of 108 shots.

For six weeks, King Richard Brodeur owned Vancouver. As the playoffs ground on, the once-discarded goalie from Longueuil, Québec, seemed unbeatable. The Brodeur trademark was to charge out of the net to face the shooter near the faceoff circle. His pads together, head up, King Richard would absorb the shot and steer the puck harmlessly into the corner.

As the Canucks waited to find out who would surface as their second-round opponent, one of the biggest upsets in Stanley Cup history was unfolding. The mighty Edmonton Oilers, the gang with Gretzky, Messier, Coffey, Kurri and Fuhr, were being taken out by the Los Angeles Kings, a team that had finished 48 points behind the Smythe Division champions. The Canucks would be spared facing the Oilers juggernaut and retain home ice advantage against the Kings.

Interest was building in Vancouver after the team's historic first series victory, but the Pacific Coliseum still had empty seats for game one of round two. The teams were tied 2–2 when, early in the third period, the Canucks fourth line chipped in with a goal. Ron Delorme, a rugged winger the Canucks had picked up in the October reverse draft, knocked over two Los Angeles players and found little Gary Lupul with a pass in the slot. Lupul knocked the puck past Kings goalie Mario Lessard for the winning goal.

Before their first sellout crowd of the post-season for game two, the Canucks and Kings traded goals. Again it was tied 2–2 in the third period, but this time Hlinka missed a wide-open net and the game went into overtime. Gradin flubbed a great chance early in the extra session, and the Canucks paid for it. A Los Angeles point shot ricocheted off Boldirev and then hit the thigh of Steve Bozek and went past a startled Brodeur. It was the first loss since Neilson had taken over as coach, and there was concern that the team's bubble had finally burst.

The Kings were revved up for game three. Playing before a rare packed house at the Fabulous Forum, Los Angeles peppered Brodeur with 18 shots in the first period. It was Vancouver that opened the scoring, however, as Campbell notched his first goal in 47 games. The Kings scored two power play goals in the second period, but a late goal by Gradin tied the game. In the third period, great individual efforts by L.A. superstar Marcel Dionne and Smyl sent the game into overtime. The game was decided in 83 seconds. Hlinka, who won 16 of 23 faceoffs that night, took the draw and slipped the puck back to Campbell. Campbell's point shot hit a Kings player on the way to the net and beat Lessard. It was a win by theft as Los Angeles outshot the Canucks 44–26.

Another sellout crowd greeted the visitors the next night, but the Canucks had more injury problems. Lindgren could barely walk and Campbell was shelved after his knee had locked overnight. But it was the Kings who broke first. After trading goals in the first period, Vancouver scored three straight goals. Los Angeles kept coming, and with 12 minutes remaining, brought the score to 4–3. Then Williams threaded a pass to Boldirev, and the smooth center made no mistake on the breakaway. The goal provided a two-goal cushion and was the winning tally in a 5–4 final score.

The Canucks hoped to finish the Kings off at home in game five, but Bernie Nicholls quieted the crowd by scoring 90 seconds into the game. Goals by Nill and Halward erased the advantage by the end of the period. Then two goals by Rota and another by Fraser in the third erased all doubts in the 5–2 victory.

Although battered through two series, the Canucks were on a genuine roll. They had lost only once in 17 games. The little guy in the Vancouver net was the key. In eight games, Brodeur had faced 282 shots and had given up only 19 goals. The fans had become believers. In the final minutes of the series-clinching victory, the first Vancouver play-off tradition started: "Na Na Na Na, Hey Hey, Goodbye" filled the rink, 16,000 voices in unison, serenading the visitors home. The city had waited a long time for a playoff run.

Vancouver opened the next series on the road, playing the Chicago Black Hawks in the league's loudest rink. The Canucks would also have to contend with legendary Tony Esposito in net, shifty forward Denis Savard and defenceman Doug Wilson, the league's hardest shooter. The series began with one of the most exciting games in Canucks history. Thomas Gradin and Terry Ruskowski exchanged goals in the first period, and then, for the next 78 minutes and 47 seconds, Chicago fans were treated to a goaltending duel of epic proportions. Through regulation time and the first overtime period, Brodeur and Esposito stoned the shooters as the play went back and forth. Chicago applied constant pressure in the second overtime, forcing Brodeur to rob both Savard and Wilson as the clock struck midnight. Finally the play switched to the Chicago end. Snepsts intercepted a puck at the point and floated a shot at the goal. In his trademark butterfly stance, Esposito made the save, but the rebound came to Nill in the slot. He roofed the puck to end what was then the longest game in Canucks history.

Two days later Brodeur was kept busy once again, facing 19 first-period shots as Vancouver was in constant penalty trouble. Trailing 3–1 in the third period, the Canucks found themselves shorthanded for the ninth time in the game. When Savard made it 4–1, Neilson decided an act of defiance was required. Before the puck was dropped at center ice, he grabbed Jim Nill's stick, took a towel off the clothesline behind the bench and began hoisting a makeshift flag of surrender. Williams, Molin and Gerry Minor joined in. As the players watched and the fans pointed, referee Bob Myers still hadn't seen the protest. Neilson sent Lindgren to tell the ref to turn around. When Myers saw what was happening on the Canucks bench, Neilson, Williams and Minor were ejected. Neilson was also fined $1000, and the team $10,000, but the ploy had taken the psychological edge off the Chicago victory.

Newspapers across North America showed photographs of Neilson and company. Back in Vancouver, a sold-out crowd armed with white towels gave the team a thunderous reception. "Towel power" was born—a playoff tradition that continues in Vancouver, but now includes rinks across the NHL.

Roger Neilson's impromptu protest enhanced the mop-haired coach's reputation as one of hockey's smartest minds. Throughout his career, Neilson became known for taking advantage of loopholes in the rules. In junior hockey, he instructed one of his defencemen to replace the goalie during penalty shots. The defenceman would rush out at the opposing forward as soon as he crossed the blue line. The tactic worked, and the league rules had to be changed to keep the goalie in net for all penalty shots.

Neilson was a workaholic and insomniac. During the hockey season he spent almost all his time at the rink, spending hours breaking down videotape of opponent's games to find trends and weaknesses. He became known as a defensive guru and was criticized for developing strategies that made the game boring. But he was also well respected by the players he coached. As the playoff run continued, the Canucks unquestionably became Neilson's team. Even after Neale had finished serving his 10-game suspension, there was no question Neilson would be behind the bench. "Why should I step in and screw it up?" said Neale about the unusual situation.

In game three, it was Chicago's turn to be frustrated by the officiating. Vancouver scored a couple of power play goals in a 4–3 victory. Savard was especially upset with the treatment he was receiving from Snepsts and the rest of the Canucks blue liners. The feisty forward spit at referee Andy van Hellemond and was ejected.

Penalties were once again a major factor in the fourth game of the series. The Canucks jumped out to a 3–0 lead, two of the goals coming on the power play, the other during a delayed penalty on Chicago. The Black Hawks fought back with a pair of goals, but Vancouver clinched the game on Halward's point shot, and Gradin added a backhander in the 5–3 victory.

The Canucks immediately took the loud Chicago crowd out of game five, as Vancouver roared out to a 3–1 first-period lead. The Black Hawks responded with some ugly stuff as tough-guy Grant Mulvey butt-ended Lindgren under the chin. Delorme challenged Mulvey, and as the two exchanged right hands, it was the Chicago player who began to wilt. Mulvey's face and white jersey were red with blood when he told Delorme he'd had enough. Chicago initiated more fisticuffs, but the Canucks were well stocked with players who could handle the rough stuff. The penalty-filled period helped set a series record with 560 minutes, surpassing the 525 minutes Toronto and Philadelphia accumulated in 1976. The game settled down in the second period as

Chicago started to take some offensive chances to solve Brodeur. The Canucks waited patiently for opportunities to counter, and finally put the game away with goals from Rota, Smyl and Boldirev. The Canucks advanced to the Stanley Cup final.

Champagne flowed in the dressing room, but in two days they would be meeting the New York Islanders, the league's best team over the regular season, who were well rested after dispatching Québec in the previous round. Led by Bryan Trottier, Mike Bossy, Denis Potvin and the combative Billy Smith in goal, the Islanders were huge favorites to beat the upstart Canucks.

Vancouver scored the first goal of the series as Gradin jabbed in a rebound past Smith. The dangerous New York power play responded, with Clark Gillies deflecting a Potvin shot past Brodeur, and then Bossy made it 2–1 on an unstoppable shot to the far corner. Gradin tied the game on a Vancouver man advantage. Just as the Canucks thought they might escape the period with a tie, Potvin scored another power play goal. Things looked bleak early in the second period as another Potvin blast with the Canucks shorthanded gave the Islanders a two-goal cushion. Smyl kept it close, and then Boldirev slipped between the New York defence to even the game.

In the third period, things settled down to a pace more suitable to the Canucks. With seven minutes remaining, Nill flipped a shot that barely dribbled past Smith into the net. Protecting a lead against the firepower of the Islanders wasn't easy. And the Canucks made things worse when Brodeur misplayed the puck and became tangled up with Snepsts. The puck came loose to a wide-open Bossy, and the game headed to overtime.

Both teams had great chances in the extra session, and with only 16 seconds left, the game seemed destined to continue into a sixth period. Off a neutral zone faceoff, the puck was dumped into the Canucks end. Brodeur settled the puck down for Snepsts. The big defenceman had been making the safe play all through the post-season—a simple shot out up the left boards and the game would continue into the second overtime. But for some reason, Snepsts looked up the middle and saw Minor calling for the puck. The pass followed, but Bossy intercepted, stopping the puck on his backhand and moving it to his forehand side in one quick, efficient motion. The resulting shot froze Brodeur, and in less than two seconds, the game was over.

Snepsts left the ice first and never came out of the dressing room to face the media. The Islanders had been surprised by Vancouver's pluck in game one. General manager Bill Torrey and coach Al Arbour complained of the Canucks "football tactics," and the New York press went to work, calling the Vancouver players thugs.

The second game was penalty-filled, but perhaps surprisingly, it was the Islanders taking most of the infractions. The Canucks gave up a shorthanded goal with Potvin in the penalty box, but buoyed by Brodeur's goaltending, Vancouver dominated the second period. The Canucks were rewarded with three goals—power play markers by Gradin and Boldirev, plus an even-strength tally by Lindgren. Bossy narrowed the margin to 3–2 before the period ended. For the second straight game, Vancouver had matched the Islanders' firepower.

Penalties were the difference in the third. Fraser was nailed for trying to start a fight, and the Islanders power play struck. Just 47 seconds later, New York took their first lead, but the Canucks quickly responded, tying the game on a Minor goal. Then Williams was penalized in a run-in with the combative Smith, and again the Islanders made Vancouver pay as Trottier took a rebound off the end boards. Bob Nystrom added insurance with less than six minutes left as New York won 6–4.

The Canucks were mad at themselves for letting two games slip away and were a tired bunch as they headed home. There were rumors that a big crowd would be waiting for them at the airport. Fire trucks raced beside the plane as it touched down, and when the players cleared customs, a crowd estimated at 30,000 was overflowing from every conceivable vantage point. It took the team bus an hour to navigate the road out of the airport.

The atmosphere inside the Pacific Coliseum was crazy for game three. The towels were out in full force, but the charged atmosphere seemed to help the Islanders, who concentrated on checking the jittery Canucks. Gillies and Bossy scored second-period goals, Nystrom added an empty-netter and the Islanders limited the Vancouver to 23 shots in the 3–0 win.

The Canucks were over their nervousness in game four, as Smyl and Butch Goring traded goals in the first period. But Bossy finished them off in the second, scoring back-to-back power play goals in a 3–1 victory. The only consolation the Canucks would be able to gain from the four-game sweep would come the following year when New York dispatched Edmonton, Gretzky and all, in four games to win their fourth-straight Stanley Cup.

The 1982 playoff run united the city and province for six exciting weeks. A downtown rally the next day attracted 100,000 fans. There may have been bigger sporting achievements in the city's history, but never had the population been held captive by the exploits of an interim coach and a group of overachieving skaters. Vancouver fans had waited 12 years for something to cheer about, and with a group of young prospects on the way, there was optimism that the Stanley Cup might return to the city for the first time since 1915.

Chapter Six

The Mighty Quinn Starts from Scratch

The organization followed a script that had been arranged the season before—Harry Neale became the new general manager and Roger Neilson was formally named head coach. Jake Milford quietly stepped aside, having literally scoured the hockey world to rebuild the Canucks.

Not surprisingly, there was a let-down after the Stanley Cup run of the previous season, or perhaps the team was playing at the level of its true talent. Whatever the case, the Canucks were below .500 at Christmas, and Neale began to make changes. In January 1983, Curt Fraser was traded to Chicago for Tony Tanti, a darting, offensively gifted forward who would become one of Vancouver's best players in the years ahead. A week later, Boldirev was also dealt to Chicago. The team slipped to third in the Smythe Division standings, five games below .500, and was dispatched quickly in the first round of the playoffs. However, Smyl, Gradin and Rota all topped 80 points, and Rota set a team record with 42 goals.

The Canucks treaded water during the 1983–84 season. In the amateur draft they selected Cam Neely, a kid out of Maple Ridge, ninth overall. Patrick Sundstrom emerged as the team's best offensive player with 91 points, and Tanti added 45 goals. Gradin and Smyl also had solid seasons. Neale continued to tinker, trading Lindgren, McCarthy and Nill. In January, he fired Neilson and took over behind the bench, guiding the team to another third-place Smythe Division finish and another first-round playoff exit.

In the off-season, the Canucks general manager took his biggest gamble, hiring 33-year-old Bill Laforge straight out of junior hockey to be the new head coach. Laforge had the reputation as a demanding, no-nonsense bench boss, and Neale hoped he would instill the work ethic the team needed. Next he traded two of the city's most popular athletes, Snepsts and Williams.

The Laforge experiment didn't last long. The Canucks struggled to a 4-14-2 start for the 1984–85 season, and Neale once again was forced to take over as coach. Despite having eight players with 20-plus goals, Vancouver slipped to fifth in the

Smythe Division and missed the playoffs for the first time in seven seasons. In June, Neale was fired. Even though he had helped guide the team that went to the 1982 Cup final, in his seven years with the team the Canucks never reached the .500 mark in the regular season.

The Canucks stayed within the organization to replace Neale, hiring assistant Jack Gordon. Gordon's legacy in Vancouver was the trade of Neely to Boston, a move that is still lamented by fans in the city. Besides being a local product, the young forward seemed to have all the tools to become an impact player in the NHL—he could shoot, skate and hit, and he was tough. Unfortunately, those skills never surfaced consistently in his short stay with the Canucks. Mired on the third and fourth lines, Neely never managed to score more than 21 goals in his three seasons on the team.

When Gordon traded away the tall, gangly kid, it repeated a pattern Vancouver had followed since selecting Dale Tallon in their first season. The Canucks would impatiently watch as their young draft picks struggled for a couple of years and then unload them just when they were ready to contribute. The Black Tuesday jinx had continued at the draft table: Michel Petit, J.J. Daigneault,

Jim Sandlak and Dan Woodley all floundered in a Vancouver uniform.

In exchange for Neely and a first-round draft pick, the Canucks received Barry Pederson. Vancouver picked up a good player in Pederson, a forward who played 12 years in the league and had consecutive 70-point seasons in a Canucks uniform. But they gave up on Cam Neely, who in his first year with the Bruins scored 36 goals. Then came three 50-goal seasons and two trips to the Stanley Cup final in a Boston uniform. More than that, Neely became an icon in Beantown, taking on the other team's tough guy, flattening defencemen with bodychecks and scoring the big goal when it was needed. To make things a little more painful, the first-round draft pick the Canucks gave up turned out to be Glen Wesley, who teamed up with Ray Bourque to give the Bruins a dynamic one-two punch on the Boston defence.

It was clear that the team needed another overhaul. Griffiths was tired of losing, and the fans were ready to wait a few years as long as the organization was making the right moves to build a solid franchise. And how do you build an NHL winner? Hire a proven hockey man, give him time and resources and then stay out of his way. It sounds simple, but it's a formula rarely followed in the musical chairs world of revolving managers in the National Hockey League.

Pat Quinn played 600 games in the league as a hard rock defenceman—133 of those in a Canucks uniform as a member of the original team back in 1970. Quinn's playing career was highlighted by one incident in his rookie season with the Toronto Maple Leafs—a thunderous bodycheck that knocked Bobby Orr out during a 1969 playoff game in Boston.

"It was scary," recalled Quinn in an interview with the *Vancouver Sun.* "Everyone, including myself, was concerned for him because he went down and didn't move. The place was deafly silent. They carried Orr off on a stretcher, and that's when the crowd got wired up. I got attacked in the penalty box. It was like a frenzy. I could feel the crowd stirring behind me. I turned around to face the crowd and raised my stick and a policeman in the penalty box grabbed me. While I was struggling with this big Boston cop, who had a strangle hold on me, we fell into the glass and it shattered, and the cop got all cut up. I dove onto the ice while the crowd chanted, 'Kill Quinn.'"

The big Irishman survived that night in Beantown and played another eight years in the league. After hanging up his skates, he worked his way

up the coaching ladder, taking over the Philadelphia Flyers in 1979. The next season he was
named Coach of the Year after guiding the Flyers
to the best record in the NHL (including a record
35-game undefeated streak) and an appearance
in the Stanley Cup final.

Two seasons later, Quinn left the Flyers to earn
a law degree. In 1984, the Los Angeles Kings
coaxed him back into coaching with the under-
standing that he would succeed Kings general
manager Rogie Vachon. In his first season with
the Kings, the team improved 23 points and
made the playoffs. Two years later, Los Angeles
failed to exercise the option on Quinn's contract
to offer him the general manager position. At
that point, the cigar-smoking Irishman decided
he would leave hockey after the season was over
to pursue a law practice. That's when Arthur
Griffiths came calling. The Canucks offered
Quinn the powers of a superboss—vice-president
and general manager. On December 24, 1986,
while still coach of the Kings, Quinn agreed to
the Vancouver job once the season was over.

Not surprisingly, the Kings cried foul because
Quinn was still under contract in Los Angeles.
The matter was brought to the league, and NHL
president John Ziegler fined the Canucks
$310,000 and suspended Quinn from coaching

until 1990. It was a harsh ruling that the Canucks successfully appealed in court.

In May 1987, Quinn assumed his managerial responsibilities and began retooling the front office. Brian Burke, a former player in the Flyers farm system and a Harvard Law School grad, was hired to assist Quinn as the director of hockey operations. Then former Flyers coach Bob McCammon was brought in as the new bench boss.

In August, Quinn began making player moves—his philosophy was to trade some of his more talented players to get two or three less prominent players in return. Patrick Sundstrom was the first to be moved. In return, the Canucks received forward Greg Adams and netminder Kirk McLean from New Jersey. The new boss told the media and fans it would take five years to build a contending team.

The Canucks had a new look to start the Quinn-led era. Gone were the Halloween uniforms, which Burke had described as "puke." The team kept the flying skate logo, this time on the front of a more traditional home white and away black jersey.

The team had a forgettable year in 1987–88, winning only 25 games to finish fifth in the Smythe Division. Adams scored 38 goals in his first season with the team and McLean replaced Brodeur as the number one goalie, but Quinn wasn't satisfied. "The one thing that disappointed me the most was that we didn't make the improvement from within, in attitudes, that I had expected," said Quinn in reviewing his first season with the team. "A losing attitude is a learned thing, and we have to unlearn some bad habits."

Before 1987 ended, the team received some good news when a judge ruled the league had overstepped its authority in the penalty imposed on the Canucks and Quinn. Both the hefty fine and coaching suspension were overturned, but Quinn remained bitter. "In my heart, that black mark will always be there and it shouldn't be," said Quinn about the affair. "It was something the league didn't like. They wanted me to be the bad guy."

The Canucks general manager overhauled the team before the next training camp began. By the time the 1988–89 season started, the team had 18 new players. One of the fresh faces was a tall, skinny junior out of Medicine Hat. With the second pick in the NHL amateur draft, the Canucks passed over some flashy stars like Jeremy Roenick, Teemu Selanne and Rod Brind'Amour to select forward Trevor Linden.

Quinn was looking for a future leader, a player to bring some stability to a franchise trying to find its place. The Canucks also made a fan-pleasing acquisition, bringing back Harold Snepsts to patrol the blue line. In need of a slick passing defenceman, Quinn acquired Paul Reinhart from Calgary. With all the new faces, it took some time for the team to come together.

Linden made an immediate impact, scoring 30 goals, and was voted by the fans as the NHL Rookie of the Year in *Hockey News* magazine. McLean helped the team give up 67 fewer goals than the year before and finished with a 20-17-3 record. Reinhart rejuvenated the Canucks power play and had 57 points in 64 games. In all, Vancouver improved its record to 33-39-8 to make the playoffs, but had to face the Calgary Flames, by far the best team in the NHL over the regular season, in the first round.

Surprisingly, the Canucks won game one in Calgary 4–3 on an overtime goal by Reinhart as McLean stopped 43 of 46 shots. The Flames came back to win the next two contests by 5–2 and 4–0 scores. In game four at the Pacific Coliseum, Linden gave the fans a taste of the clutch play he would provide in the coming years, scoring a goal and adding three assists in a 5–3 win. Game five in Calgary was a write-off as the Canucks were outshot

40–18 in a 4–0 loss. Two nights later at the Pacific Coliseum, Vancouver's four-goal second period forced a deciding game back at the Saddledome. In game seven, the Canucks came back from 2–1 and 3–2 deficits to force overtime. Mike Vernon became part of Flames folklore when he made a great breakaway save off of Stan Smyl in the extra session. With only 39 seconds left in the first overtime, Jim Peplinski banked a puck off of Joel Otto's skate past a surprised McLean.

It was a tough way to lose a series. The Canucks had shown surprising grit in handling the rough play of the bigger Calgary forwards. After the Flames went on to win the Stanley Cup, several players said the Vancouver series was their biggest hurdle. And despite the loss to Calgary, it had been a strong finish and Vancouver put itself back on the hockey map. The organization was well represented with finalists for three major trophies. Linden was second for the Calder Trophy as the top rookie, McLean was third in the voting for the Vezina Trophy as top goalie and McCammon was runner-up as coach of the year.

In July 1989, the Canucks organization made the front of sports pages across Canada with the announcement that Soviet star forward Igor Larionov had signed a contract with the team. The project had taken four years of negotiations with the Soviet Ice Hockey Federation as the Griffiths family enlisted the help of Senator Ray Perrault. Two months later, Vancouver signed his line-mate Vladimir Krutov. The Canucks had wrapped up the services of two-thirds of the KLM line, one of the most feared offensive forces in inter-national hockey (Sergei Makarov signed in Cal-gary). In bringing Larionov and Krutov to Vancouver, Quinn was gambling that the Soviet stars would be able to adjust quickly to NHL-style hockey and upgrade an offence that had scored the fewest goals in the league. It was an expen-sive venture. Both players signed three-year deals worth $375,000 per season, plus the Canucks would have to pay an equal amount to Sovinter-sport, the organization that negotiated transfer fees.

There was an immediate impact at the box office as season ticket sales jumped by 3500 and the crowd average went up to 15,400 from 13,700. On the ice, the team took a step backward, fin-ishing fifth in the Smythe Division and out of the playoffs. Krutov was a one-season bust, showing up at training camp in terrible shape and never recovering. Larionov's game improved as the sea-son went on, and his friendly manner made for a comfortable fit with his teammates and with the fans. One bright spot came after the season ended. The Canucks hosted the 1990 NHL entry draft at BC Place. The event was free of charge, and a record 19,127 fans showed up to cheer as Quinn announced that the Canucks would take Petr Nedved second overall.

In 1990–91, Vancouver improved by one point, which was enough to squeak into the playoffs. Quinn fired McCammon halfway through the season and took over as coach. The Canucks were eliminated in the post-season by Los Angeles in six games.

The Vancouver general manager and coach was starting to take some heat from hockey fans in the city. He had just completed five years as the team's boss, and the Canucks seemed to be going nowhere. Things can change quickly in professional sports. A little Irish luck, a fortunate trade or two and the arrival of the Canucks' first superstar were all that were required to bring the franchise to a new level of success.

Chapter Seven

The Arrival of the Russian Rocket

November 5, 1991: high up above the ice surface at the Pacific Coliseum, Jim Robson was in his customary broadcast location. Just like the sold-out crowd below him, the voice of the Canucks was eager to see what would happen when Pavel Bure came over the boards for the first time. The fresh-faced Russian was about to play his first NHL game against the Winnipeg Jets, and everyone was eager to find out if the young forward with the impressive press clippings was ready for the big leagues.

He answered the question in an instant. "In his first shift he sifted through everyone on the ice," recalled Robson, a play-by-play radio and television announcer for 2000 NHL games between 1970 and his retirement in 1999. "In one shift, he electrified the building and created an excitement that built through the game. He won the Vancouver fans over on his first NHL shift."

In that first on-ice appearance, Bure not only impressed 16,143 fans with his skills, but also with the speed at which operated, plus his total dedication to attacking the Jets defence. In that first game against Winnipeg, number 10 didn't score a goal or record an assist; he didn't even pick up a penalty. But after the game, he was the only topic of discussion.

The replays of that night's memorable debut highlighted a second-period rush. Bure collected the puck in his own zone and immediately zoomed up the ice, zigzagging around a couple of Winnipeg forwards in the neutral zone. Just as he reached the Jets blue line in top gear, he lost control of the puck. Before the fans could groan, Bure pulled his skate back and kicked the puck up to his stick. The Winnipeg defence was frozen by his high-speed recovery, and he burst through with only the netminder to beat. A couple of rapid-fire dekes followed, but the goalie foiled Bure's scoring try with a close-in save. The rookie tumbled into the boards, and the fans were on their feet for the first of many standing ovations that would mark his time in the city.

Bure's amazing debut changed the face of Vancouver sports for the next eight years. It also provided the Canucks broadcaster with the opportunity to describe the heroics of a home-team superstar for the first time. "As a broadcaster, it was like having a big homerun player in baseball. Every shift you wondered if he was going to score," said Robson. "And not only was it the goals, but it was the way he scored spectacular goals. There was a lot of attention focused on him all the time."

Bure's amazing journey as a Vancouver Canuck started on June 17, 1989. The amateur draft was underway. Pavel Bure was considered the most talented player, but his availability was doubtful. In those days, drafting young Soviet players was a huge risk. Only older players were being released to go to the NHL, and hockey experts believed Bure wouldn't be allowed to leave for several years. As the draft proceeded, Bure was bypassed in the first three rounds. At that time, there was a rule restricting the drafting of under-age (under 19) European players after the third round unless they had played at least 11 games at their country's elite level for two successive seasons. According to NHL records, the young Russian had played only five games for the Central Army team in 1987–88, six fewer than required.

Vancouver management believed otherwise, and chief scout Mike Penny pushed Pat Quinn to take a gamble on drafting Bure. Penny had been on an overseas scouting trip in Europe during the 1987–88 season and knew Bure had played some extra games—four with the Central Army team and two more in exhibition games with the Soviet national team. As the Canucks waited for their turn in the sixth round, Penny tried to convince Quinn that Bure was eligible for selection. There was no doubting that Bure was a top prospect. During the 1988–89 season, he had been Rookie of the Year in the Soviet Elite League. At the World Junior Championship in Anchorage, he led the Soviets to a gold medal, scoring eight goals on a line with future NHL stars Sergei Fedorov and Alexander Mogilny. Finally the Canucks general manager relented, and NHL vice president Brian O'Neill announced, "The Vancouver Canucks select Pavel Bure of the Soviet Union."

Several teams who were considering drafting Bure rushed to the table to protest his eligibility. After formal complaints from two teams, the NHL announced an inquiry would take place. It took league president John Ziegler 11 months to decide that the Canucks' selection of Bure was illegal and that he would be made eligible for the draft in 1990, during which he could be claimed by any team in any round.

The Canucks decided to appeal the decision, but had only a month to prepare their case before the 1990 entry draft got underway. Quinn put in a call to Igor Larionov, who was back in Moscow, to see if he could find any documents that would prove Bure had played 11 games in 1987–88. A Russian journalist did some digging for Larionov and found that Bure had played in extra exhibition games and a club tournament—all totaled, he had seen action in 12 games that season. Larionov had the documents verified by the Soviet Ice Hockey Federation and faxed them off to Quinn. On the eve of the draft on June 15, Ziegler reversed his ruling, and the Canucks were allowed to keep the rights to Bure.

Over the 1989–90 and 1990–91 seasons, older Russian stars were allowed to play for NHL teams. Among them were Larionov and Krutov for the Canucks. This led to some speculation that Bure might be released too, but the defections of Mogilny in 1989 and Fedorov in 1990 made it unlikely that the Soviets would let Bure, their most talented prospect, leave. In 1991, Bure was part of the Soviet team that played at the World Junior Championship in Saskatoon. Security was tight as the Soviets feared more defections. Bure led all players with 12 goals in the tournament. In an interview with *Toronto Sun* reporter Tim Wharnsby, the Russian said he'd never defect because he was concerned that his brother Valeri, a top hockey prospect, would be punished by Soviet officials if he left.

In the summer of 1991, Bure, who was still the property of the Central Army hockey team, refused to sign a three-year contract extension, so Soviet officials kept him off the roster to play in the Canada Cup. On September 6, 1991, Pavel Bure, his brother Valeri and his father Vladimir boarded a plane to Los Angeles. Their visas said they'd be gone a month, but it was clear that their goal was a chance at the NHL. In mid-September, Vancouver hockey fans were made aware of Bure's arrival in North America. Before a contract could be sorted out, the Canucks would have to get clearance from the NHL on whether his contract with the Central Army team was binding. Ziegler ruled that the contract was valid.

Vancouver management moved slowly during the weeks that Bure stayed in L.A. They were still fuming over having to pay Vladimir Krutov $800,000 to buy him out of the remaining years in his contract. Bure decided to get things moving by launching a lawsuit against the Soviet Ice Hockey Federation, claiming his original contract was signed under duress because he was threatened with a posting in Siberia. The Soviets responded formally to the complaint, which legally allowed the Canucks to offer Bure a conditional contract.

After two weeks of tough bargaining, the Canucks worked out a deal with Bure's agent, Ron Salcer. Before a judge in a Detroit courtroom, the Soviets and the Canucks also came to an agreement. For a $250,000 transfer fee, Pavel Bure was finally going to play in a Canucks uniform. In the coming days, the Vancouver media found out that Bure had signed a four-year deal worth just over $3 million, which made him the second-highest paid player on the team behind Trevor Linden. Quinn was optimistic about the deal. "Everyone is still a prospect until they can do it here," said Quinn after signing Bure to his first NHL contract. "At this point he's a prospect, but a great prospect. Many people in hockey say he's a world-class player. Now we have to consider how we'll develop his talent. We hope it won't upset the chemistry of our team."

The mystery and intrigue of the entire Bure caper launched a sense of anticipation that no other player had brought to the franchise. He was mobbed after his first practice when 2000 fans came out to a small community rink to watch him skate. Scalpers were out in full force for his November debut, doubling and tripling the value of tickets. After the Winnipeg game, which ended in a 2–2 tie, Ian MacIntyre of the *Vancouver Sun* wrote, "If Winnipeg are the Jets, then what do you call Pavel Bure? How about the Rocket?" The name stuck; the Russian Rocket had arrived.

With Bure in the lineup, the Canucks went on a seven-game undefeated streak. He picked up his first goal in his fourth game, a backhander that helped Vancouver demolish Los Angeles 8–2. A quarter of the way through the season, the Canucks had the best record in the NHL.

Lost in the arrival of the 20-year-old Russian was the coming together of Quinn's team. McLean continued to develop as a top goalie. The defence was rebuilt, except for Doug Lidster, who had been drafted by the team and had become their most consistent blue liner. Jyrki Lumme had been a steal in a 1990 trade with Montreal, as Quinn gave up only a second-round draft pick. Gerald Diduck was added a year later, again from Montreal for just a fourth-round pick. The biggest move Quinn made was just before the trade deadline in March 1991. The Canucks parted with hard-rock defenceman Garth Butcher and their leading scorer Dan Quinn to add forwards Cliff Ronning, Geoff Courtnall and Sergio Momesso, plus defenceman Robert Dirk. The trade gave the team some depth at forward, joining Trevor Linden, Greg Adams, Igor Larionov, Petr Nedved, Gino Odjick and Garry Valk. Big Dana Murzyn came from Calgary, and then

Dave Babych was added in the off-season. Midway through the 1991–92 season, Quinn lured veteran Randy Gregg, a five-time Stanley Cup champion, out of retirement for extra insurance.

Bure was the big weapon the team needed to complement a deep roster of talent. Quinn moved Bure to a line with Larionov that reawakened the veteran Russian's scoring touch. By the end of December 1991, the Canucks had a 10-point cushion atop the Smythe Division. Bure was making opposition defencemen look silly with his speed, but the rookie had trouble finishing off his plays, usually getting in too close on the opposing goaltender.

Vancouver kept cruising along, setting a team record with 42 wins and 96 points, the fourth-best record in the league. The Canucks had improved by 31 points and had met Quinn's five-year deadline in becoming a league power. Bure had also found his scoring touch. In the team's last 23 games, the Russian Rocket scored 22 goals. He finished with 34 goals in his rookie campaign, despite playing in only 65 games.

Bure would now get his first taste of playoff hockey against the Winnipeg Jets. The scoring machine suddenly went cold and Vancouver struggled, falling behind 3–2 in the series. In game six, the offence came alive as Bure scored three times in an 8–3 shellacking. Vancouver won the deciding game 5–0 and advanced to face the Edmonton Oilers.

Edmonton was determined to shut Bure down, and they had the league's most annoying player, Esa Tikkanen, to do the job. For six games, the talkative Finn was all over the young Russian— tugging, jabbing, grabbing, pushing and shoving. Bure managed only one goal and one assist as the Canucks were eliminated in six games.

In June, Bure won the Calder Trophy as the league's Rookie of the Year, the first award ever won by a Canuck player. Quinn was named NHL Coach of the Year.

There was no sophomore jinx the next season. Larionov's departure to Switzerland did not slow Bure down as he scored 20 goals in the team's first 20 games. The forward with the teen idol looks had become Vancouver's most popular athlete. "Pavelmania" was a huge adjustment for the introverted Russian. He had to move twice into more secure residences to escape groupies. In November, *Sports Illustrated* sent a writer to profile Bure, confirming his popularity had extended outside the Lower Mainland. The attention didn't bother Bure's performance on the ice or the club's winning record. On March 1, he scored his 50th goal of the season, the first Canuck to reach that milestone. He finished the 1992–93 season with 60 goals and 50 assists, becoming the first Vancouver player to score more than 100 points.

The team also steamed ahead to set new club records, including an 18-game home unbeaten streak. Despite a mini-slump in the last weeks of the season, the Canucks finished with 101 points, a new franchise record, and repeated as Smythe Division champions. They had scored 364 goals, another team record, and had four players with 30 or more goals.

For the second straight season, Vancouver was matched against Winnipeg in the first round of the playoffs. The Canucks won the opening two games on home ice as Linden led the team with his physical play and faceoff domination. The Jets rebounded to take the third game, but in game four, Vancouver took control of the series with a 3–1 win. Back at home, the Canucks failed to close things out and let a 3–1 lead slip away. A fluke goal by rookie sensation Teemu Selanne completed the game five comeback as the Jets won 4–3 in overtime. But Vancouver won the series in Winnipeg in a wild game that saw the home team take the lead three times, only to have the Canucks answer back. Adams scored the clincher in overtime, and Vancouver moved on to face the Los Angeles Kings.

The Canucks won the opener at home against Gretzky's gang by a 5–2 score, but then dropped four of the next five games. It was a high-scoring series, as the Kings took advantage of turnovers and penalties to seemingly score at will in their 6–3 and 7–4 games two and three victories. In the fourth game, Vancouver scored six unanswered goals in a 7–2 laugher. Pivotal game five was extended into overtime by a late third-period goal by Linden. In overtime, with the Canucks defence caught out of position, a little-known rookie named Gary Shuchuk beat McLean. Only sensational goaltending kept Vancouver in the deciding contest. The Canucks were outshot 50–23, but actually led 2–1 in the second period. Los Angeles scored two power play goals to regain the advantage and never looked back. Despite having superior depth and size, Vancouver looked slow against the Kings, who would lose to Montréal in the Stanley Cup final.

Vancouver fans were especially incensed at Nedved after the final game ended. The young Czech asked Gretzky for his stick as a souvenir and skated off the ice with a big smile on his face. The gesture symbolized the ease with which the Canucks were willing to accept defeat in the play-offs. Quinn made it clear that he had higher expectations for his team.

Chapter Eight

So Close... Another Run For the Cup

After the team's disappointing playoff run the year before, the theme to start the 1993–94 season wasn't about who the Canucks had added, but rather who they had lost. Jim Sandlak, Ryan Walter, Garry Valk and Doug Lidster were gone because of trades or retirement. Unsigned Petr Nedved was a hold-out in the Czech Republic. Vancouver would be part of the Pacific Division to start the season, a mostly cosmetic change as all the divisions were renamed into geographic designations.

The Canucks started the year on a roll, winning six of their first seven games, led by Bure's 13 points. Vancouver management was trying to work out a new contract with their superstar forward, but things had stalled. George McPhee, the Canucks' assistant general manager, was as tough a negotiator as his predecessor, Brian Burke (who had left the team to work as Gary

Bettman's assistant in the NHL front office). As the season rolled on, Bure became more upset with the hard line of the Canucks. He suffered a groin injury in October and missed eight games. The team faltered, and even when Bure returned, the club remained inconsistent. Injuries were part of the problem as five regulars were out of the lineup.

In January, Ronning went down with a shoulder injury, forcing Quinn to add some scoring depth. In two deals, Vancouver picked up forwards Jimmy Carson from Los Angeles and Martin Gelinas from Québec. On March 4, St. Louis secretly signed Nedved to a contract. Because the young forward was a restricted free agent, the Canucks were awarded forward Craig Janney and a second-round draft pick as compensation. The only problem was that Janney refused to report to Vancouver. The Canucks and Blues started talking again, and just before the trade deadline, Janney was dealt back to St. Louis for defencemen Jeff Brown and Bret Hedican, plus rookie forward Nathan LaFayette. Vancouver continued to stall around the .500 mark all season, comfortably in second place in their division, but well behind the Calgary Flames.

The injury that had slowed Bure down earlier in the season was only a memory as the regular season came to an end. The Russian Rocket led the NHL with 60 goals and finished fifth in points with 107. Bure had scored 154 goals in three seasons—only Bossy and Gretzky had started their careers with higher totals.

The first round of the playoffs would be another tilt against the Calgary Flames. Most observers agreed that the Canucks could match the talent level of their hated rivals, but would fold again as in the early rounds of past playoffs. Surprisingly, the Canucks dumped the Flames 5–0 in game one in Calgary as McLean stopped 31 shots. The next game was a sloppy, penalty-filled affair, with the Canucks making more mistakes than the Flames and losing 7–5. Game three was a tighter-checking contest, as the game remained scoreless until the third period. Calgary scored first, then the Canucks tied it on a Momesso goal, but a Theoren Fleury slapshot beat McLean. Gary Roberts scored a late Calgary marker, and the Canucks never recovered in the 4–2 loss.

Vancouver was predictably desperate to tie the series at home in game four and outplayed Calgary in the first two periods, but led only 2–1. As was the case through most of the regular season, the Canucks were unable to put a whole game together. Poor defensive coverage allowed the Flames to even the score early in the third period.

A few minutes later, McLean failed to clear the puck; Calgary intercepted and Fleury made them pay with the winning goal.

Vancouver was in bad shape heading back to the Saddledome for game five. An injury to forward Murray Craven forced Quinn to shake up his lines; Linden was moved to center between the struggling Bure and Adams. The Canucks coach looked like a genius as Bure one-timed an Adams pass to go up 1–0. Calgary tied the game, but McLean wouldn't break the rest of the way. In overtime, Vancouver took advantage of a rare Flames mistake as Courtnall picked up a loose puck at center ice, roared down the wing and beat Calgary goalie Mike Vernon with a slapper into the top corner.

Back at home in game six, Vancouver was able to carve out a 2–1 second-period lead. Calgary took over the play and was rewarded with the equalizer, but McLean wouldn't wilt. The game went into overtime, and the Flames made another blunder—a bench minor for too many men on the ice. The Canucks capitalized when Linden converted a Bure rebound.

The seventh game was back in Calgary, with the local press putting lots of heat on the Flames for allowing the Canucks back in the series. Fleury gave the home side an early lead, but Bure replied quickly on the power play. Courtnall scored a few minutes later, and despite being outplayed, Vancouver had a 2–1 lead after 20 minutes. The Flames dominated the second period and managed to pop two goals behind McLean. In the third period, Calgary checked the Canucks to a standstill, allowing only three shots on Vernon. With hope fading and only four minutes remaining, Adams took a pass from Bure and charged toward the net, lifting a backhand that barely trickled into the net. For the third-straight game, the teams would battle each other in overtime.

Both teams had great chances in the first extra period, but it was Kirk McLean who etched himself into team history with what simply became known as "The Save." The play started with a bad pinch by Murzyn. With only Lumme back, the Flames came in on a three-on-one—Fleury with the puck, Robert Reichel on the wing and Roberts as the trailing forward. The talented Fleury held and held the puck, freezing Lumme and McLean and then, at the last moment, feathering a wonderful pass to Reichel. The Czech forward didn't hesitate, one-timing Fleury's pass with a wicked shot that looked to be headed into the wide-open net. The goal judge anticipated a goal and turned the red light on, but McLean had other ideas. In desperation he stretched out, throwing himself feet first across the crease. His toe made contact with the puck and it stayed out.

The Canucks had survived the first overtime. McLean's save was an initial hint of providence; maybe this underachieving group would be given the opportunity to come together as a team. Perhaps it could be 1982 all over again. But unlike the Cup run 12 years earlier, this edition of the Canucks could match the talent level of any of their opponents.

In the early moments of the second overtime period, Brown made eye contact with Bure as he skated away from a Calgary checker. Brown snapped a long pass through the middle that landed right on Bure's stick. The Russian Rocket took off, beating the floundering Flames defence with pure speed. Then came a goal-scorer's move—a fake to the backhand, then over to the forehand around the outstretched body of Mike Vernon, waiting, waiting and then carefully depositing the puck into the net. And that was it. The Saddledome crowd was silent; the Canucks were mobbing each other on the ice. It was a series victory by the narrowest of margins, but it couldn't have been sweeter.

Next came the Dallas Stars, a well-rested group that had swept the St. Louis Blues in four games. Vancouver surprised the home team by jumping out to a 4–1 lead, but Dallas came back to tie the game. The Canucks scored the winner off a face-off when LaFayette got the puck to Gelinas. Linden added an empty-netter in the 6–4 win.

Bure was at his best in Vancouver's 3–0 victory in game two. He scored two goals—the last one a Stars killer. With 21 seconds left in the second period, Bure intercepted a pass in the neutral zone, zoomed around defenceman Derian Hatcher and then, while barely holding his skate edge, snapped a shot over goalie Andy Moog. In the first period, the Russian also showed his combative side. Dallas had been paying extra attention to Bure, throwing in an extra jab, push and slash when they could get away with it. Bure extracted some revenge when he threw an elbow into the face of giant defenceman Shane Churla. It was a knockout blow to the Stars tough guy, and although Bure was later fined, he was not suspended.

The series shifted back to Vancouver, and when the home team went up 2–0, it looked like Dallas would be steamrolled. Instead, the Stars scored four straight goals and shut down the Canucks in a 4–3 win. Game four would be the pivotal contest. Linden opened the scoring, but Dallas replied in the second. The goaltenders held the third period scoreless, sending the game into overtime.

Momesso ended it. The big guy with the permanent scowl broke out of a long slump to bang the puck in from close range.

Two nights later, the Stars were eliminated in a 4–2 loss. Bure scored the winning goal on a breakaway late in the third period. The Adams-Linden-Bure line overcame the normally tight-checking Stars to notch 10 goals and eight assists in five games. The path to the Stanley Cup final would now take the Canucks to Toronto to face the Maple Leafs.

Toronto assigned their top checking unit to stop the Linden line, and for most of three periods, the strategy worked as the Maple Leafs led 2–1. With 1:42 left, a Leafs penalty coupled with Quinn pulling McLean for an extra attacker gave Vancouver a two-man advantage. Linden broke through the Toronto defence to beat Felix Potvin with a backhander, sending game one into overtime. Late in first session after Potvin stopped Bure on a breakaway, McLean attempted to clear the puck out of the corner. Peter Zezel intercepted the puck and flipped a shot at the net, beating McLean, who didn't have time to recover from his foray into the corner.

In game two, Bure was back to skating, dazzling the Leafs with his full repertoire of dekes and moves. Late in the first period, he put the

Canucks on the scoreboard. Intercepting a clearing attempt in the Toronto zone, Bure zipped around a defenceman before whipping a shot into the top corner. The game went back and forth, with the Maple Leafs scoring three times on the power play. Late in the third period, Vancouver won the game with the man advantage. Linden found Lumme open in the slot—Lumme's shot went through Potvin to tie the series.

As the teams flew across the country to get ready for the third game, Vancouver fans were enjoying their second prolonged trip through the playoff marathon. The East-West rivalry was in full gear—sports columnists from both cities were ripping into each other. The towels were out again at the Pacific Coliseum, and when Bure drew first blood on a partial breakaway, the ensuing roar could be heard up and down Renfrew Street. After Adams put the Canucks ahead 2–0, Bure was sent on a clear breakaway from center ice. The Russian forcefully stuffed the puck through Potvin's pads. A power play goal by Gelinas late in the game sealed the 4–0 victory.

Toronto tried to reverse Vancouver's momentum in game four, but McLean turned away all 20 shots in the first two periods. With two minutes remaining, Cliff Ronning connected on a two-on-one break with Momesso. Bure added the empty-netter, and McLean had his second straight shutout in the 2–0 victory. The Canucks were one win away from the final.

The Maple Leafs weren't willing to go down without a fight and at one point held a 3–0 lead in game five. Goals by Craven, LaFayette and Adams tied the game. The goalies took over through the third period and the first overtime session. Only 14 seconds into the second over-time, Babych's wrist shot handcuffed Potvin. The Leafs goalie couldn't handle the rebound, and Adams was waiting at the edge of the crease. For the second time in Canucks history, Vancouver would be fighting for the Stanley Cup.

On May 31, 1994, the Canucks faced off against the New York Rangers at Madison Square Garden. While Vancouver had shaken aside a disappointing regular season to reach their potential as a talented hockey team in the post-season, the Rangers were battling the demons of a 54-year Stanley Cup drought and the turmoil of a team coached by Mike Keenan.

Iron Mike had taunted and confronted his players over the course of a 52-win season. Mark Messier had kept the team together on the ice as the Rangers survived an intense seven-game series against New Jersey. The Rangers captain had promised a New York victory over the Devils

led Leetch with a jarring bodycheck. Against
run of the play, New York tied the score when
Lean let Leetch's weak flip shot deflect off
into the net. The turning point came late in
first period when, on a Canucks power play,
re clipped defenceman Jay Wells with a high
ck. The contact drew blood, and referee Andy
n Hellemond issued Bure the most severe pen-
y possible, a five-minute major plus a game
sconduct for deliberately causing injury. The
ll hushed the crowd, and a minute later,
e deflated Canucks gave up a power play goal
Anderson. The Rangers then coasted to a 5–1
cision.

Game four featured the same high tempo
ckey as the Canucks jumped ahead 2–0 on
als by Linden and Ronning. Leetch scored his
th goal of the playoffs when the Rangers were
orthanded. Two minutes later, the all-star
fenceman tripped up Bure, and a penalty shot
as awarded. It was only the sixth penalty
ot opportunity awarded in Stanley Cup final
story. As Bure collected the puck at center ice,
chter rushed out and then gradually faded
ck to his net. Bure went to the same move that
d beat Mike Vernon in the Calgary series, but
e acrobatic Richter smothered the forehand
ke with his right pad. It was a crucial save,
lowing the Rangers time to tie the score on the

in the sixth game of the series and then delivered
with three goals and an assist in a 4–2 win. Two
nights later, New York advanced to the final with
a 2–1 overtime decision.

The Rangers were loaded with six ex-Edmon-
ton Oilers—Messier, Glenn Anderson, Esa Tikkanen, Kevin Lowe, Craig MacTavish and Adam
Graves, who had all won Cups. New York had
perhaps the best offensive defenceman in hockey
with Brian Leetch, and American-born Mike
Richter had been a standout in net all season.
The 27-point regular season gap between the two
teams made the Rangers the consensus favorite
with hockey writers. But then there was the Kirk
McLean factor. The Canucks goalie had responded
with game-saving performances against three
different teams; the Rangers were next.

From the opening faceoff in the first game,
New York swarmed the Vancouver zone and was
rewarded with a Steve Larmer goal three minutes in. McLean weathered the storm, kicking
out one shot after another. Early in the third
period, Hedican scored his first goal in 147 games
to even things. New York fans came to life again
three minutes later when Alexei Kovalev beat
McLean off a set-up by Leetch. Vancouver was
unable to crack through the Rangers' checking
wall, but with a minute remaining, Ronning

fired an innocent shot from a sharp angle that Gelinas was somehow able to tip under Richter's arm.

In overtime, New York fired 17 shots at McLean. Captain Kirk's body or equipment got in the way of all Rangers attempts. In the last minute, Leetch beat McLean with a rising shot that clanged off the crossbar and came to Bure at his own blue line. The counter-punching Canucks started up the ice; Bure found Ronning with a pass that started a two-on-one with Adams. The pint-sized center waited for Adams to get open and then laid the puck over in perfect position for the one-timer. Adams' shot went over Richter's shoulder, and Vancouver had a series lead.

The New York press peppered McLean with questions after the game. The Vancouver net-minder had stopped 52 of 54 shots, the second most in Stanley Cup final history. There was talk of the Rangers hex; already there was doubt that New York could finish off their Stanley Cup quest.

Messier and company dominated the action again in game two, but both teams exchanged goals in the first period. Linden made a rare mis-take in the second period. His risky pass was picked off by Messier and then converted by Anderson. Still, the Canucks had several chances

to tie the score in the third period—ning and Adams all hit the crossbar. V pulled McLean in the final minute attacker, Richter stopped Gelinas in Leetch's empty-netter ended the sus

In the first two games, Bure had down by a combination of the flu an ers' checking. A Toronto newspap reported that Bure's agent, Ron threatened to have the Russian Ro playoff games in an effort to pressure into agreeing to finalize a new con and the Canucks denied the accusa the Vancouver press started to pic story, Salcer admitted that just before Bure had signed a new deal with reported five-year agreement wortl lion.

The off-ice distractions didn't see the Russian star in game three. Pla a charged-up crowd at the Pacific Co den found Bure with a lead pass ju into the game, and Bure's 15-foot s past Richter. The Rangers were a st Vancouver, twice taking penalties t the Rocket. The Canucks were also Messier and Graves, thumping thei The Canucks faithful went crazy

power play before the second period ended. Richter was sharp in the third, keeping the Canucks off the score sheet. As overtime loomed, the New York power play capitalized again when Leetch set up Kovalev for the game winner. Larmer's long shot deflected off Babych with less than three minutes remaining to provide the insurance marker in the 4–2 win.

New York was on the verge of a victory celebration, but in game five, the Rangers were the nervous team. The crowd at Madison Square Garden kept chanting, "We want the Cup," but the only goal after two periods was a Jeff Brown slapshot that blew by Richter. Everyone expected Vancouver to protect their one-goal cushion, but in one of the craziest periods in Cup final history, the Canucks increased their lead to 3–0 on goals by Courtnall and Bure. In the next six minutes, the Rangers answered back on goals by the ex-Canuck Doug Lidster, Larmer and Messier. The Garden crowd was going nuts, but before they could sit down, Babych scored on a bad-angle shot. Three minutes later Courtnall converted a rebound, and a minute later Bure tucked in another goal. Eight goals in 12:38 of hockey—the series would return to Vancouver.

Pat Quinn had looked to match Linden against Messier throughout the series. In the early going the Canucks captain seemed star struck, but as the games marched on, Linden began to assert his will on the series. The most dominant player, shift after shift, however, was Leetch. Fearless on the rush, Leetch kept finding openings, and Vancouver was seemingly unable to cover him.

The folks at home were ready for game six. The Pacific Coliseum had never hosted anything as exciting, and the Canucks players fed off the crowd. Vancouver stormed the Rangers through the first period, but had only Brown's power play goal to show for their efforts. The suddenly hot Courtnall doubled the advantage to 2–0, but Kovalev narrowed the deficit before the second period ended. The score stayed 2–1 until, with 12 minutes left in the third period, Linden set up Brown at the point. His blast sifted through a bevy of players and past a startled Richter. It looked like the Canucks were going to force a deciding seventh game. Then, with two minutes left, LaFayette set up Courtnall in the slot for a backhander that seemed to beat Richter high to the corner, just inside the crossbar. The crowd thought Courtnall had scored, but the play continued. Bure missed the net with the rebound, and Leetch gathered the puck and started back the other way. A pass from Leetch to Anderson, a pass from Anderson to Messier, and the puck was in the Vancouver net.

The Canucks protested, asking referee Bill McCreary to consult with the video-replay officials. If the Courtnall shot was ruled a goal, Vancouver had the game; if not, Messier's would count, and the score would be at 3–2 with still a minute left. After a long delay, McCreary pointed toward center ice, indicating a goal, and the crowd erupted—the series was tied.

There had been only 10 game sevens in the 56 Stanley Cup finals leading up to June 14, 1994. Before a frenzied crowd at Madison Square Garden, the Vancouver–New York finale surpassed the expectations of hockey pundits across North America. It was a classic. The marvelous Leetch scored first, 11 minutes into the first period, on a set-up from Messier and Sergei Zubov. Less than four minutes later, the dangerous Rangers power play made it 2–0, this time on a shot by Graves. Linden made the Garden crowd jittery five minutes into the second period, scoring a shorthanded breakaway goal. Eight minutes later, New York's power play responded as Messier restored the two-goal lead. The period ended with the Rangers leading 3–1.

The Canucks would need an early third period goal to get back in the game, and Linden delivered. At the 4:50 mark, the Canucks captain took a pass from Courtnall and whizzed a shot past

Richter. The power play marker put the Rangers on their heels. Linden almost completed the hat-trick, but Richter kicked out a low backhand that was on target for the corner. Ronning had a great chance, and then, with six minutes left, Court-nall found LaFayette uncovered in the slot. The rookie forward's one-timer had Richter beaten, but with a loud clang, the puck nailed the goal-post and stayed out. The Rangers took no chances the rest of the way, icing the puck at every oppor-tunity and relying on savvy and experience to keep Vancouver at bay. The 1993–94 season came to an end on a MacTavish faceoff win, and the Rangers won the Cup.

"I thought going into this game we were des-tined to win," said Quinn later. "Our guys worked as hard as they could and came up short. To lose a series like that tears your guts out. But my heart is full of pride for these guys."

The entertainment value of the seven-game drama was reflected in the TV ratings. The American numbers set a new record for hockey, and on the Canadian side, the game seven rat-ings were the highest for any hockey game since the Canada-Russia Summit Series in 1972.

Brian Leetch won the Conn Smythe Trophy as the playoff MVP. Leetch finished with 11 goals and 23 assists to lead post-season scorers with 34 points. He also led in plus/minus ratings with +19. Pavel Bure finished with 16 goals, the most in the playoffs, and 15 assists for 31 points, second behind Leetch. Linden was second in Canucks scoring with 25 points.

For the Griffiths family, the Cup run was symbolic of how far the organization had come from past seasons where fans had to endure both ineptitude on the ice and in the front office. Frank Griffiths, his health fading, had passed the responsibility of running the team to his son Arthur, who in turn had pushed for the hiring of Quinn. "The playoff run was tremendously gratifying," recalled Arthur Griffiths after the season ended. "As an organization, we've always wanted to bring respectability and competitive performance to the community, and we were ecstatic we were able to reward our fans, many of whom we made during the playoffs. The highs were as high as you can get in sport, with the exception maybe of one goalpost."

The people of New York embraced their new champions with a joyous, noisy, yet peaceful celebration. In Vancouver, things turned ugly. Through their playoff journey, Canucks supporters had chosen the trendy Robson Street shopping district as the public gathering spot to celebrate wins. An aggressive, hostile atmosphere took over in the early evening hours after the game ended. An estimated 70,000 people had come downtown, and many of them unleashed their frustration by overturning cars and breaking store windows. The police were caught off guard, and by the time reinforcements arrived, a full riot was underway. On newscasts across North America, people watched images of police using batons, dogs and tear gas to battle rioters in the streets of Vancouver. By the time order was restored, 200 people had been injured, dozens were arrested and a 19-year-old man was on life support after a rubber bullet had penetrated his skull.

It was a signal that Vancouver had grown up into a big city with big city issues. The innocence of the 1982 Cup final, when Canucks fans celebrated the efforts of their flawed, yet overachieving warriors, had been replaced a dozen years later by higher expectations that their more talented heroes had not fulfilled. Vancouver had hosted a world exposition in 1986, and the city had been discovered. Vancouver was no longer a backwater; it was now described as a "world class city." The Vancouver Canucks had come agonizingly close, but had not delivered a championship. Second best was no longer good enough.

Chapter Nine

New Owner, New Home, New Problems

Two days after the 1994 Cup final ended, with businesses still replacing their store windows on Robson Street, the Canucks formally announced the signing of Pavel Bure to a five-year contract worth $25 million, making him the third-highest-paid player in the league behind Wayne Gretzky and Mario Lemieux. It was a smart business decision. Arthur Griffiths had announced that the Canucks were to play in a new $165 million rink downtown and that the family's sports empire would be expanded to include an NBA expansion franchise. Locking up the 23-year-old to a long-term contract was key in making sure the corporate community bought the high-priced executive boxes and club seating that were so important to a team's revenue stream.

Pat Quinn decided that it was time to turn the head coaching job over to Rick Ley, his top assistant, so he could focus more on his duties as general manager. It was a risky decision—Quinn had a locker room charisma that few coaches could match. The low-key Ley would have to battle to establish a similar presence while taking over a team that would be returning off the disappointing results of a Cup final.

A larger drama was unfolding in the sports pages through the summer. After failing to come to a collective agreement with the Players' Association, the owners shut the league down before the regular season could get started. The main issue was the owners' insistence on a new salary-cap system to slow down the increase in players' salaries. The impasse threatened the entire season, but finally the lockout ended on January 12 with a six-year agreement.

A 48-game season was announced, with the teams playing opponents only within their conference. Vancouver would open their season against the Dallas Stars on January 20, but as the team's mini training camp wrapped up, there was some concern about Bure's status. His agent, Ron Salcer, insisted the team pay Bure's salary during the time missed with the lockout. Canucks management disagreed, and the Russian winger stayed away. With the season opener looming, a compromise was reached—the team would set the money aside and try to work out a settlement at a later date.

The lockout, Bure's situation, contract battles with other players and a new coach were not the ingredients for a happy, family-type atmosphere within the organization. Even the fans were testy; the team had raised ticket prices and had lost 1000 season ticket holders.

On the ice, the team started slowly with a 9-13-8 record. Inspired outings were interrupted by long stretches of listless hockey. One of the few bright spots was the play of rookie forward Mike Peca. The wiry forward quickly established a reputation as one of the league's best open-ice hitters when he caught Winnipeg star Teemu Selanne with a devastating check at center ice. Unfortunately, the collision also broke Peca's cheekbone, and he was forced to miss several weeks of action.

On March 7, 1995, Arthur Griffiths called a news conference to announce his family was selling their majority interest of the team, the new stadium and the NBA Vancouver Grizzlies to a Seattle-based cellular phone tycoon named John McCaw Jr. The Griffiths family was forced to sell after the combined debt of their sports empire overextended their finances. Arthur Griffiths would stay on as the chairman and CEO, but the team was no longer locally owned.

The tone of the new regime was established at the first news conference—McCaw didn't show up. The family shunned the media, rarely giving interviews or letting their photos be taken. Owning a couple of sports franchises hadn't changed anything.

Pat Quinn didn't let working for a new boss distract him from trying to improve the team. In danger of missing the playoffs for the first time in four years, the general manager made four deals at the trade deadline. Greg Adams, Jiri Slegr, Gerald Diduck and Nathan LaFayette were gone. Russ Courtnall (Geoff's younger brother) and goalie Corey Hirsch were in—the other players involved were prospects or draft picks.

Vancouver sputtered through the shortened regular season with an 18-18-2 record, good enough for sixth in their conference. Bure led the team in scoring for the third straight year, but with only 20 goals and 23 assists in 48 games, he had dropped out of the top 10 in league scoring.

The Canucks were matched against third-place St. Louis in the first round and again had to face a Keenan-coached team; Iron Mike had joined the Blues after a contract battle with the Rangers. Vancouver was once again the underdog. Keenan had signed four former Rangers and had a solid team led by Brendan Shanahan, Brett Hull, Al MacInnis and goalie Curtis Joseph.

St. Louis won the opener on home ice; two power play goals in the first period were all the Blues needed in a 2–1 victory. The Canucks trailed 2–0 early in game two, but thanks to Russ Courtnall's hat-trick and a shorthanded break-away goal by Bure, Vancouver charged back to win 5–3.

The white towels were out again for game three at the Pacific Coliseum, even though the rink was 3000 fans short of a sell-out. Ronning and Bure each assisted on three goals in an easy 6–1 victory. The city began to rev-up again, antic-ipating another post-season run. The Coliseum was full for game four, and the Canucks responded with Bure whizzing around the ice and Linden banging into Blues. Vancouver's defence was struggling with injuries, however, and St. Louis took advantage of several miscues to score three goals in a four-minute span in the second period. The Blues evened the series with a 5–3 decision.

The Canucks survived more mistakes in game five, giving up four leads before Ronning notched the 6–5 winner in overtime. St. Louis was almost as sloppy as Vancouver, giving up five short-handed goals in the first five games of the series.

Another capacity crowd expected the Canucks to put the Blues away in game six. Instead, Vancouver didn't show up, losing 8–2. For the first time since 1992, McLean was pulled after giving up six goals through two periods.

Over 20,000 fans filled the rink in St. Louis to watch game seven. The Canucks had the early jump, taking a 2–0 lead on rookie defenceman Adrian Aucoin's first playoff goal and another shorthanded marker by Bure. The Blues owned the second period, but McLean allowed only one goal in the 25 shots he faced. Geoff Courtnall restored the two-goal advantage before the period ended. Early in the third, Ronning made it 4–1, then the Blues scored twice to make it interesting, but Bure's empty-netter assured the Vancouver victory. The Russian winger had made up for an uninspired regular season by setting team records of seven goals and five assists in one series.

Next up were the Chicago Blackhawks, who had also survived a tough seven-game series against Toronto. The Blackhawks had an all-star goalie in Ed Belfour, the deepest defence corps in the league led by Chris Chelios, and star forwards Jeremy Roenick, Tony Amonte and Denis Savard.

Chicago's four-game sweep of the Canucks included three overtime thrillers. The magic of the previous year's run had been replaced by frustration. Vancouver's blue line injuries caught up to the team as the Canucks were unable to hold on to leads in three of the four games. Bure suffered a rib injury in the third period of game four and didn't return. When Chelios scored the series-winning goal in overtime, it was the end of the last NHL game at the Pacific Coliseum. There was no tribute to the Canucks' first home as the fans quietly filed out of the rink. Disappointment, not nostalgia, ruled the day. Expectations had been raised again about a team that a year earlier had been only one game shy of the Stanley Cup.

What next? With a solid core group of players—Bure, Linden, McLean and Lumme—all in their prime, Quinn was looking for one more impact player to get the team back as an NHL power. On July 8, 1995, hockey pundits all agreed the Vancouver general manager had pulled it off. The Canucks acquired Alexander Mogilny from the Buffalo Sabres for Peca, junior defenceman Mike Wilson and a first-round draft pick.

By adding another $3.7 million to their payroll, the Canucks acquired one of the league's best snipers. In 1992–93, the Russian winger had scored 76 goals—teamed with Bure, Vancouver would have the most dangerous one-two punch in hockey. The plan was to re-unite the pair who, along with center Sergei Fedorov, had made up the Soviet national team's most dangerous line in the early 1990s.

Vancouver had assembled the most talented team in its history to coincide with the opening of the new arena, GM Place. Season ticket requests began to pour in after the trade was announced. The Canucks had 18,422 seats to fill every night, which included 88 executive suites and 2195 high-priced "club seats." The $165 million sports palace had all the bells and whistles—posh restaurants, an oversized scoreboard and a state-of-the-art sound system. The new downtown arena was a hit. The Canucks, as part of the newly named Orca Bay Sports and Entertainment corporate entity, sold out 28 games in their first season at GM Place, drawing a new franchise record 729,629 fans.

And what about on the ice? Vancouver was scoring lots of goals as everyone expected, but their sloppy defensive play was hindering a rise in the standings. Ley benched Brown to send a message to his defencemen. Things became much worse on November 9. During a game in Chicago Stadium, Bure was hit by Blackhawks defenceman Steve Smith. The collision tore the anterior cruciate ligament (ACL) in his right knee. Surgery was required, followed by six to nine months of rehab. Bure was gone for the season. The Canucks promptly fell into a funk, winning only one of their next eight games. Quinn traded a second-round pick to get Esa Tikkanen from New Jersey, and Brown was sent to Hartford for a couple of minor leaguers. Led by the scoring of Mogilny and a career season by Linden, the Canucks were hanging onto a playoff spot.

In March, Vancouver sent first-round draft pick Alek Stojanov to Pittsburgh for another underachieving first-rounder, Markus Naslund, a deal that would later prove to be one of the most important in the club's history. Down the stretch, rookie Corey Hirsch took over from a slumping McLean as the team's number one goalie. With six games remaining in the regular schedule and under tremendous pressure to ensure the Canucks qualified for the post-season, Quinn fired Ley and reinserted himself behind the bench. Vancouver didn't play any better with Quinn back, but they managed to nudge into the playoffs with a 32-35-15 record. Mogilny had a banner year with 55 goals, third best in the league, and 52 assists for 107 points. Linden finished with 33 goals and 47 assists for 80 points, and four other Canucks managed at least 20 goals.

The Canucks faced the Colorado Avalanche in the first round of the 1996 playoffs. In Joe Sakic and Peter Forsberg, the Avalanche had the best one-two punch at center in the league. The mid-season acquisition of goaltender Patrick Roy from Montreal made them Stanley Cup contenders. The most surprising part about Vancouver's series loss to Colorado was that Quinn bypassed McLean to start Hirsch in five of the six games.

The Canucks gave the Avalanche quite a tussle. With the series tied at 2–2, Vancouver was ahead 3–2 in the fifth game when, with only six minutes left, Sakic scored a power play goal to even things up. The Colorado captain then added the winner in overtime. In game six it was again "Burnaby Joe" who did the Canucks in, scoring the winning goal with less than two minutes remaining. The Avalanche went on to win the Stanley Cup, and according to Colorado coach Marc Crawford, it was Vancouver that gave his team the stiffest challenge. It had still been another disappointing season for Canucks fans; little did they know that things would only get worse.

Chapter Ten

Turmoil

A recipe for a disastrous season: start with a rookie head coach with no professional coaching experience, add a superstar trying to regain his form after major knee surgery, throw in a significant injury to your team's captain who had previously never missed a game and, oh yeah—play an entire year without a top-caliber NHL center.

That was a condensed version of 1996–97. In the off-season, Quinn went looking for a new coach and hired highly regarded Tom Renney from the Canadian Olympic program. Renney's resume included a Memorial Cup championship in Kamloops and a silver medal at the 1994 Olympics. He was also a young, media-friendly coach who Quinn hoped would provide a welcome contrast to Ley's crusty style.

Pavel Bure came to training camp in high gear, anxious to return to pre-injury form. In the pre-season he proved to disbelievers that he was back. In a game against Boston, the Russian Rocket intercepted a pass while the Canucks were shorthanded. Zooming away from all-star defenceman Ray Bourque, Bure moved in on the Bruins goalie, let the puck go into his skates, and then in one fluid movement, kicked the puck back onto his stick and deposited it in the net. The goal was shown again and again in television highlight packages across North America.

Canucks fans were optimistic that with their superstar back and healthy, they would return to form as a contending team. Vancouver opened the season with a 3–1 win, but in the third period, Bure was pushed awkwardly into the end boards. Despite being able to partially brace himself against the impact, the Russian's head still hit the boards. Bure continued to play, but his game lacked its usual sharpness; many observers felt he had suffered a mild concussion.

In November, without much fanfare, Arthur Griffiths sold his remaining interest in the Canucks to John McCaw—the team was now fully American-owned. On the ice, Vancouver was playing better and holding onto a playoff position. Then the injuries came—six regulars went out. The most serious loss was a December 1 injury to Linden. The Canucks captain strained knee ligaments, breaking his ironman streak of 482 games. In all, Linden would play in only 49 games in the 1996–97 campaign. By the end of December, the team had slipped to ninth in the conference. Without Linden in the lineup, Vancouver lacked a first-line center to play with Mogilny and Bure. For the rest of the season, the team was wildly inconsistent, winning three or four games in a row before going on another tailspin.

In March, the Canucks lost 11 out of 15 games to fall out of the playoff race for good. Bure finally disclosed that the hit he suffered in the first game had resulted in lingering pain that increased as the season progressed. He was finally put on the injury list and played in only 63 games with a disappointing 23 goals and 32 assists. The team finished five games under .500 and four points out of the playoffs. For the first time in seven years, the Canucks did not go to the post-season.

Then things got worse. It didn't seem that way at first. In July, at a splashy news conference in Vancouver, Mark Messier pulled a Canucks jersey over his head (with the new Orca Bay killer whale logo), signing a three-year contract worth $20 million. Adding the future Hall of Fame player seemed like a no-brainer: he would provide leadership and give the team the number one center they so badly needed. The signing showed the players and fans that the Canucks were determined to win the Stanley Cup. "In acquiring Mark, we have added to our talent base and our core of leadership," said Quinn. "The intangibles Mark brings will allow us to get a little closer to our dream and our goal, which is to win the Stanley Cup." But the addition of the former captain of both the Rangers and Oilers also came with some significant risks. He was 36 years old, had become injury-prone and, in the 1997 playoffs, looked like an old man when he was matched up against Philadelphia's star, Eric Lindros.

A string of issues plagued Messier's time in Vancouver. First up was the controversy over his jersey number. Messier had worn number 11 throughout his career, but no Vancouver player had chosen the number in respect to the late Wayne Maki, an original Canuck who had passed away. The number was never officially retired, allowing Messier to claim it. The Maki family went public with their displeasure, and many fans joined in to protest the decision.

The next issue was the captaincy. The press had dubbed Messier as "the greatest leader in team sports," but Trevor Linden had served as the captain for several years and was in his prime as a player. Messier down-played any controversy, saying that Linden should remain the captain. Still, hockey writers wondered how the team could remain harmonious with two such strong personalities. Just before the season opener in Tokyo against the Anaheim Mighty Ducks (the teams were in Japan to promote the NHL's participation in the Nagano Olympics), Linden announced that he was relinquishing the captaincy to Messier. Linden said the decision was entirely his own and that he didn't want the issue to become a distraction through the year. It was a gracious move by the classy forward, but it only addressed one of the potential distractions to start the year.

The press reported that Bure had asked the team to trade him—a culmination of years of frustration with the Canucks management. The Russian Rocket denied the stories, but when Bure fired his agent, it only seemed to accelerate the rumours. Local sportswriters began to question his commitment to the team. Bure, however, was the best Canuck player when the season started and developed an instant on-ice rapport with Messier. The other Russian superstar, Mogilny, was not on the ice; he was holding out in a contract dispute with the team after Quinn had been unable to trade him during the summer.

Lost in the all the off-ice drama was the addition of Swedish rookie blue liner Mattias Ohlund, who would become the Canucks' best defenceman as the season progressed, and goalie Arturs Irbe, a free-agent signing who would push out Kirk McLean as the top netminder.

After a .500 start through their first eight games of the 1997–98 season, the Canucks lost seven straight. On November 4, Orca Bay management announced that after 11 seasons, Pat Quinn had been fired. It was a shocker. Most of the media covering the team thought that Renney would have been the first to go. It also seemed the decision had been made without a backup plan, as the team named no successor to Quinn. The 54-year-old said he was shocked by the decision, but with a $32 million payroll, the Canucks had been the league's biggest underachievers. Just days before the firing, Quinn admitted things would have to change or his job could be in jeopardy. "I get assessed all the time," said Quinn after another loss. "You think our owner wants to make the investment he's made and see these results?"

By the end of his tenure, Quinn's surly responses to tough questions had alienated much of the media. Fans criticized the lack of depth in the farm system and poor decisions at the draft.

Most of all, the perception was that Quinn had assembled a team full of overpaid slackers and that someone was needed to bring accountability back to the franchise. Nine days later, with the team struggling with a 4-13-2 record, management announced the firing of Renney and the hiring of Mike Keenan as the new head coach.

Despite winning the Stanley Cup in New York and taking two other teams to the Cup final, Iron Mike had lasted only two-and-a-half years in St. Louis. As the general manager and coach of the Blues, Keenan had dismantled the team, bringing in 82 different players in his short tenure. In the process, he had feuded with or traded almost all his star players—Wayne Gretzky, Brett Hull, Brendan Shanahan and Curtis Joseph—while becoming just as unpopular with the fans and media. Vancouver sportswriters anticipated a soap opera–type atmosphere in the coming weeks, and the fiery Keenan didn't disappoint.

At first, the change provided the required spark. The team signed Mogilny to a new contract, and Keenan put the two Russians together with Messier to form a super line. Bure was happy to get more ice time, and his relationship with the team improved when management quietly agreed to pay him $1 million of his lockout back-pay. The team began to put some wins together.

A month later, things fell apart. After winning only two of 14 games in December, Keenan publicly criticized the effort of Linden and cut his ice time. Several players, some on the record, some anonymously, responded by voicing their displeasure with Keenan. Messier was put in an awkward situation; as the captain of the team he had to have the respect of the other players, but from their days together in New York, he was also loyal to Keenan. Messier stuck with the coach. Keenan was given the authority to make trades, and the housecleaning began. In a little under three months, Iron Mike made nine trades. McLean and Gelinas, both Linden supporters, were the first to go in a trade to Carolina. Odjick, the tough enforcer who was also Bure's closest friend, was sent to the Islanders, and Babych was shipped out to Philadelphia. The shocker came on February 6, when Linden was traded to the Islanders for forward Todd Bertuzzi and defenceman Bryan McCabe. The former captain had become such a fixture in the community, with his many charitable efforts, that it seemed a given he would stay with the team until his retirement, much like Stan Smyl. But under Keenan's watch, Linden needed a fresh start. The team was now Messier's to lead.

There were only four players left—Bure, Murzyn, Hedican and Lumme—from the 1994 Stanley Cup final team. The Canucks finished the season with 64 points, last in the Western Conference. Bure had a strong comeback campaign. His 51 goals were one behind the league leader's, and he placed fourth in scoring with 91 points. Messier was next with 60 points in his first tumultuous season in Vancouver. Ohlund was named to the league's All-Rookie team.

Orca Bay moved quickly to get the Canucks on track again. In June 1998, Brian Burke signed a three-year contract to take over as general manager on the condition that Keenan would get to stay as coach. After serving as Quinn's assistant in Vancouver for several seasons, Burke had finished a five-year stint as the NHL vice president in charge of league discipline. His first challenge was to keep Bure in Vancouver. Rumours persisted that the forward wanted a trade, and in August, he went public with his request to be moved. Burke asked for patience to get a deal done, but Bure insisted that he would not play with the team again even though he had a year left on his contract. Burke suspended him without pay.

Without the Russian Rocket in the lineup, few fans predicted the Canucks would go very far as the 1998–99 season started. In an effort to cut down on their losses (which management had said were $36 million the previous year), Vancouver also let Lumme go to free agency. Surprisingly, new goalie Garth Snow kept the team around .500 in the first few months of the season.

The sweepstakes for Bure dragged on as Burke fielded offers for the superstar. The team, suffering injuries to Bertuzzi and Mogilny, began to slide. Finally, on January 17, 1999, a deal was finalized. Bure, Hedican, junior defenceman Brad Ference and a third-round draft pick were traded to Florida for defenceman Ed Jovanovski, forward Dave Gagner, minor-league goalie prospect Kevin Weekes, junior forward Mike Brown and Florida's first-round draft pick in either 1999 or 2000. It didn't end up being the flashy deal that many had predicted. For seven years, Bure had dazzled Vancouver fans like no other player. The relationship had run hot and cold in that time, but it was never boring. Burke had traded the franchise's greatest player as an investment for the future. It was a sad day for many Canucks followers.

A week after the deal, Burke fired Keenan and brought in Marc Crawford, an ex-Canuck from the 1982 Cup run who had coached Colorado to a Stanley Cup in 1996. The team played out the rest of the season in uninspired fashion, winning

only 20 games and finishing last in the conference once again. After three successive seasons
of averaging 17,000 or more fans, attendance
dipped to 15,803 at GM Place.

Out of the chaos, a new scorer emerged.
Naslund was put on a line with Messier, and the
talented left winger responded with 36 goals and
30 assists to lead the team. It was rebuilding time
once again, and Canucks fans had to have faith
that Burke, Crawford and company could get the
job done.

Chapter Eleven

The Burke Years

With the departure of Pavel Bure, the team lost not only its greatest player, but also its most exciting. Whether it was the initial "Pavelmania," his legion of female admirers, the intrigue associated with his alleged ties to the Russian mob or the seclusion he sought away from the rink, Bure had an aura of mystery and magnetism that sold tickets and kept the team as a hot topic of discussion.

In an odd turnaround, a middle-aged New Englander with reddish hair, beefy cheeks and a tough-guy scowl replaced Bure as the focal point of the Vancouver franchise. In his seven years with the team, he feuded with the media, challenged the loyalty of the fans, criticized the league and badmouthed some of his players. There was no middle ground with Brian Burke— fans in the city either loved him or hated him.

Burke was pugnacious by nature. After serving as team captain for the Providence College team, he was signed by the Philadelphia Flyers and assigned to their farm team in Maine. His Irish temper served him well as an under-skilled but fearless player with the Calder Cup–winning Mariners in 1977–78. Realizing that an NHL career would be a long shot, Burke gained acceptance to Harvard Law School and, after graduating, became a player agent for six years in the Boston area.

Burke made the jump to the NHL in 1992 as the general manager of the Hartford Whalers. His stint with the Whalers lasted only a couple of years. When Pat Quinn took over the Canucks in 1987, he hired Burke to negotiate player contracts, run the farm system and head up the scouting department. For the next five years, he served as Quinn's assistant until taking a job with the NHL as an assistant to league president Gary Bettman. As the vice-president in charge of league discipline, Burke handed out player suspensions for the next five seasons.

Upon his return to Vancouver, Burke had a mess to clean up. On top of the inferior on-ice product, the fan base had deteriorated. The Canucks had one of the biggest payrolls in hockey, but with the team's poor performance came lots of empty seats. Much of Vancouver's corporate community had also pulled its support. There was no direction within the organization.

Brian Burke was hired to change all this in a hurry. He was in tough at the outset with Bure's trade demand. Burke waited six long months to finally pull the trigger on the deal with Florida. In getting Jovanovski from the Panthers, Burke had landed a young defenceman who had been a standout in his rookie season, helping Florida get to the Stanley Cup final. He was tough, a great skater with lots of offensive potential. The deal also fit in with another of Burke's mandates—to shrink the team's $36 million loss. Shedding Bure's salary helped the Canucks general manager bring next season's shortfall down to $15 million.

Burke's decision to hire Marc Crawford as the new coach was a statement on what type of hockey the Canucks would play. Burke and Crawford wanted an exciting, up-tempo style, not the defensive trap system that the New Jersey Devils had perfected on the way to a Stanley Cup in 1995 and continued to use with success. With a smaller budget, Burke knew the organization would have to develop more of its own talent. The team's farm system was shaken up, and the scouting department was given more resources. Coaches on the farm team were instructed to teach the same system that Crawford was using with the big team, making it easier for call-ups to make the transition to the NHL level.

On the morning of June 26, 1999, just before the entry draft was about to begin, Burke made deals with Chicago and Tampa Bay to get two choices in the top three. With the picks, Vancouver selected twin brothers Daniel and Henrik Sedin from MoDo of the Swedish Elite League. "That's the hardest deal I've ever made, the most work I've ever put into a trade," Burke recalled. "They told us they weren't coming [to the NHL] unless we got them both. It was seminal moment in Vancouver. We had 7600 season tickets, and that's when I think the media in Vancouver started to take us seriously." Burke's wheeling and dealing at the draft grabbed attention around the league, but the payoff for Vancouver hockey fans would have to wait, as the twins decided to stay in Sweden for the upcoming season.

The 1999–2000 campaign started slowly for the Canucks as Crawford began to implement his system. In December, Burke traded three players to get goalie Felix Potvin from the New York Islanders. Three months later, in a trade partially motivated to trim payroll, Mogilny was sent to New Jersey for Brendan Morrison and Denis Pederson. With Potvin as the number one goalie and the rest of the team coming together under Crawford, the Canucks finished the season on a 15-12-5 roll to improve to 30-37-15, a jump of 25 points over the previous season. Playing on a line with Messier, Naslund again led the team in scoring with 65 points. Bertuzzi showed promise with 25 goals and was named the team's most exciting player. Ohlund and Jovanovski continued to develop on the Canucks blue line.

The most memorable moment of the season was unfortunately also one of the most sickening in the team's history. On February 21 in a game at GM Place against Boston, Bruins tough guy Marty McSorley took a two-handed swing with his hockey stick that caught Canucks enforcer Donald Brashear on the right side of his head. The blow stunned Brashear. He fell heavily, the back of his head hitting the ice twice with enough force to dislodge his helmet. The Vancouver forward suffered a concussion but recovered in time to finish the season.

The two heavyweights had had several encounters over the years, with 28-year-old Brashear gaining the upper hand in the most recent fights against 37-year-old McSorley. Earlier in the game, McSorley had lost again to the Vancouver player and later tried to goad him into another battle. With seconds left in the hockey game and the Canucks leading 5–2, McSorley suddenly lashed out with his stick as Brashear skated in front of the Bruins defenceman. McSorley was banned from the league for a year, effectively ending his playing career. In October 2000, he was convicted of assault with a deadly weapon and received an 18-month conditional sentence.

Despite the team's improvement in 1999–2000, the repeated theme of rebuilding for next season had taken its toll on the franchise. The season ticket base had shrunk to 7000, and an average of only 14,649 fans had shown up for the games. Burke realized he had a lot of work ahead to convince the city the Canucks were on the right track. He began getting the team more involved in the community, and players made frequent appearances at fundraisers and other events. Burke hosted town meetings, met with season ticket holders and attended business gatherings. It was a grassroots approach to reattach the team to the city.

Then, in more dramatic fashion, Burke tried a little shock therapy to wake up the Canucks faithful. At a news conference to pressure the federal government to provide financial assistance to the Canadian teams, he held up a coin and said that all it would take to move the Canucks was "one quarter and a phone booth."

The Canucks boss had pushed a hot button. Two Canadian teams, the Winnipeg Jets and the Québec Nordiques, had already relocated to American markets. For many fans, Burke's remarks felt like blackmail. After all, the Canucks had compiled one of the lowest winning percentages in NHL history, and only two improbable runs to the Stanley Cup final had provided a reprieve from the team's mediocrity. Over most of those long, unsuccessful seasons, Vancouver fans had filled the rink. Burke's comments were never forgiven by many of the team's supporters.

As the 2000–01 hockey year began, the Canucks did not have Mark Messier in the lineup. Burke saved $6 million by not picking up the option year in the captain's contract. For most fans, Messier's stay in Vancouver was symbolic of the team's decline. Burke disagreed, stating Messier had played a pivotal role helping the younger players like Naslund (the new captain) develop.

The team's turnaround continued. The Sedins made their debut, and Daniel chipped in with 20 goals in his rookie season. Jovanovski had his best offensive totals with 47 points. Burke felt the team needed an upgrade in goal. In February he traded for Dan Cloutier, a young netminder from Tampa Bay. A month later, with the team cruising into the playoffs, Naslund broke his leg in an innocent-looking play in a game against Buffalo. The team slumped without their captain, winning only three of 13 games down the stretch. But led by Naslund's 41 goals and with significant offensive contributions from Bertuzzi, Morrison and Andrew Cassels, the Canucks jumped to 90 points and earned a playoff spot for the first time in four seasons. Vancouver was swept by Colorado in four games in the first round.

Still, the season was considered a success. Vancouver had taken another positive step in reaching the playoffs, and average attendance jumped to 17,017 with 17 sell-outs. The rebuilding of the team had also taken place within the context of severe cost-cutting by Burke. The Canucks general manager, along with assistant Dave Nonis, were relentless in their negotiations with players to keep their salary structure in place.

The team's fortunes continued to ease upward. In November, the general manager increased his popularity by giving up a first-round draft pick to bring Trevor Linden back to Vancouver. The former captain's offensive production had declined, but Burke felt his veteran presence was needed in the young lineup. The Canucks improved by a modest four points in 2001–02, with a record of 42-33-7. After Christmas, Vancouver went 28-9-3 for a league-leading percentage of .721. Naslund had 40 goals and 50 assists to lead the team in scoring. He was also named a league first team All-Star—an honour last accomplished by Bure. Naslund's line-mate, Bertuzzi, had a breakout season with 36 goals and 49 assists. A combination of strength, speed and soft hands, the giant power forward had finally reached his potential as a dominating player. Morrison also proved to be a valuable addition as the center between the star wingers, contributing 67 points. For the first time in the team's history, Vancouver led the NHL in goal scoring—a testament to the wide-open, entertaining style of hockey that Burke and Crawford promised the fans.

The Canucks were definite underdogs against powerhouse Detroit in the first round of the playoffs. Led by Bertuzzi's physical presence and solid goaltending by Cloutier, who stopped 64 of 69 shots, Vancouver shocked the Red Wings with 4–3 and 5–2 victories in Detroit. Towel power was back for game three at GM Place. The Canucks were more than holding their own when, in the final moments of the second period, Cloutier misplayed Nicklas Lidstrom's 100-foot shot from center ice—a whiff that ended up becoming the game-winning goal. The Red Wings took advantage of Vancouver's fragile confidence and won the series with four straight victories. The Naslund-Morrison-Bertuzzi line struggled, collecting just eight points in the six games; Naslund had only two points. Cloutier was pulled in the last two losses, giving up bad goals early in each game.

It was an awful way for the young goaltender to end the season. Cloutier had been marvelous in 62 regular season games, with a 31-22-5 record, a goals-against average of 2.43 and seven shutouts. Little did Canucks fans know that this was just the start of Cloutier's misfortune in the post-season.

Even though the team had lost to the much more experienced Red Wings, with their $68 million payroll, Detroit coach Scotty Bowman praised the direction the Canucks were taking. "I told Marc Crawford, you've got a good young team and I hope you can keep them together because they're entertaining. It was no fluke that we lost two games," said the game's all-time most-winning coach.

More improvement was expected to start the 2002–03 season. In September, after a nasty contract battle between Burke and prospect Peter Schaefer, the Canucks general manager shipped the promising forward to Ottawa for defenceman Sami Salo. In November, the team added more depth to the blue line by acquiring Marek Malik from Carolina. With Ohlund, Jovanovski, Brent

Sopel and Murray Baron, the Canucks had one of the deepest defence contingents in the league.

The Naslund-Morrison-Bertuzzi line became the most dangerous trio of forwards in hockey. Naslund stayed at the top of the league's scoring race for most of the season with 48 goals and 56 assists for 104 points, losing the title by two points on the last day of the season to boyhood friend Peter Forsberg in Colorado. Bertuzzi set new personal marks with 46 goals and 51 assists for 97 points, while Morrison added 25 goals and 46 assists for 71 points.

As a team, the Canucks had long winning streaks in November and January to improve their record for the fourth consecutive season. Vancouver set a club standard with 104 points on a 45-24-13 record. The Canucks had all the ingredients to become a top-tier team. They had a scoring line, plus some forward depth with the Sedins, Linden and Matt Cooke. The defence was big and, led by Jovanovski, could add some goals. Cloutier had another strong season in goal with a 33-16-7 record and a goals-against average of 2.42.

On the final day of the regular season, the Canucks lost to the inferior Los Angeles Kings, allowing Colorado to edge Vancouver for first place in the Northwest Division. Naslund held back nothing in telling the fans after the game that the team had choked, while promising a better playoff performance. In the first round, the suddenly tight Vancouver squad fell behind the St. Louis Blues three games to one.

Bertuzzi had been the Canucks' best player. In game two, he knocked Al MacInnis out of the series with a crushing check into the corner-boards, separating the all-star defenceman's right shoulder. The loss of MacInnis, the NHL's top-scoring blue liner, and a bad case of the flu began to weaken the Blues. The Canucks came back to win the next two games. In game seven, Bertuzzi leveled defenceman Bryce Salvador with another devastating check. St. Louis looked scared every time the hulking winger was on the ice, and the Canucks took over the game to win the series.

In the Western Conference semi-final, Vancouver was matched against the Minnesota Wild, a maddeningly efficient defensive club coached by the guru of the trap, Jacques Lemaire. The Wild were effective when they waited for other teams to make a mistake—then they would launch a deadly counterattack led by their young superstar, Marian Gaborik.

The Canucks took control of the series with a 3–1 lead, including two overtime wins. It seemed like at long last, the team was ready to re-engage Vancouver fans with a long playoff run. In a not-so-smart move, the press played up a comment from Bertuzzi, who told Minnesota fans lined up to buy tickets to game six of the series that they were wasting their time because the Canucks would win game five at home. The games had all been close. Minnesota still felt with a bounce or two they could get back in the series, and with the extra motivation provided by Bertuzzi's comment, the Wild won the next two games. Back at GM Place for game seven, the Canucks went ahead 2–0, but Minnesota came back with four unanswered goals to win 4–2. In 210 playoff series with a team up 3–1, only 20 teams had come back to win three straight. Vancouver did it in the first round; they let it happen in the second.

It was a crushing disappointment, but Burke evaluated the collapse as part of young team's maturation to reach the next level. He defended the performance of Cloutier and the other Vancouver stars and declared that the core of the team would be kept together. Methodically, Burke and Nonis signed all their key players to contract extensions—Vancouver management believed their team could make a run for the Stanley Cup.

Chapter Twelve

The Nightmare Season

The talented Vancouver team Brian Burke had put together was determined to make amends for the previous season's disappointment. The Canucks were quietly efficient through the 2003–04 campaign, playing .500 or better hockey through each month.

Dan Cloutier, the most frequent target of the fans for the team's post-season woes, had another solid season—a 33-21-7 record and a goals-against average of 2.27. In their fourth year in the league, the Sedins emerged as second-line offensive threats. Both players had career best point totals (Daniel with 54, Henrik with 42). The Naslund-Morrison-Bertuzzi line was still terrorizing opposing goalies, though Bertuzzi's numbers were down, and, more worrying at times, the big forward seemed uninterested in the game around him. Still, fans at GM Place were entertained most nights by a deep team with a ton of talent.

The first distraction came in February. In an interview, Burke described himself as a "lame duck GM," referring to his status as not having a contract with the team after the season ended. There were rumours that the candid Irishman with a shamrock tattoo on his hip had a fractious relationship with his employers at Orca Bay, especially CEO Stan McCammon. During the dark days of the post-Keenan Canucks, Burke's courting of the media had been instrumental in raising the team's standing with the public. His straight-shooting approach and colourful quotes, combined with the team's improved performance each year, had made him an icon in the city. His "lame duck" declaration seemed to make his future in Vancouver uncertain. Sportswriters speculated that Burke was banking on his personal popularity to keep his job. It was a big gamble. Unless the team had a strong playoff performance, Burke's poor post-season resume could be justified as a reason to let him go, despite the wondrous turnaround he had made with the franchise, both as a competitive team and as a financial moneymaker. Local call-in shows and newspaper editorials took strong positions that Burke should be re-signed. McCammon was forced to comment, saying only that Orca Bay would deal with Burke's contract at the end of the season. For a time, the Burke story pushed the team's performance to the sidelines.

Then, on February 16, an on-ice explosion of sorts would start a chain of events that turned a year so full of promise into a nightmare. Late in a game in Colorado against the Avalanche, the Canucks were nursing a 1–0 lead. Markus Naslund was stretching for a loose puck when forward Steve Moore swerved into him at high speed, striking him with his shoulder and arm. Naslund never saw the hit coming. He went down hard; his head clanged off the unforgiving ice, cutting him and knocking him out.

Vancouver's most valuable player had suffered a concussion, a jagged cut on his forehead and a hyper-extended elbow. The hit was questionable. The referees didn't penalize Moore on the play, and a review by the league backed the officials' decision. Whether the hit was legal or not, hockey pundits debated whether the Avalanche forward should have stepped into Naslund while he was vulnerable. The code of letting up when a player was dangerously exposed seemed long removed from the game. Concussions to star players like Naslund were becoming more common, and the league hadn't stepped in to protect its most valuable assets.

The usual bland and guarded comments of a post-game locker room were replaced by some emotional declarations by the Canucks. Brian

Burke, the former NHL vice president responsible for player suspensions, was critical of Moore's decision to go after his team's best player. "Whether it's an elbow or not, it's clearly a head-hunting shot on a star player by a marginal player," said Burke. "It's obvious the player dropped down to get him at head level. This was a chance to take out a star player and he took it."

Crawford was upset that no penalty was called on the play. "From the view that we had—and it was right in front of the bench—it looked like [Moore] knew what he was doing. And it was a vicious hit, and a vicious hit against a star player should not be tolerated."

The most incendiary statement came from tough forward Brad May, who said there would be a bounty on Moore's head the next time Colorado faced the Canucks. Bertuzzi was also clear that there would be retribution for the hit. For his part, the 25-year-old Moore said he was finishing his check and didn't even know it was Naslund that he was taking out.

Suffering a grade two concussion, Naslund was expected to be out of action for two weeks, but after a quick recovery, he ended up missing only three games. The rematch against Colorado came on March 3, with the Swedish forward back in the lineup. Both teams had been warned that no nonsense would be tolerated by the league, and with NHL commissioner Gary Bettman in the stands, the anticipated fireworks never materialized. The Canucks came back from a two-goal deficit to tie the Avalanche 5–5. Canucks tough guy Wade Brookbank took on Avs policeman Peter Worrell, and Bertuzzi went after Colorado's Adam Foote, but Moore was not involved in any of the fisticuffs. Naslund had a goal and two assists in the rough but exciting hockey game.

With the first rematch out of the way, fans wondered if the next meeting between the teams five days later at GM Place would be less intense. The atmosphere turned from raucous to ugly as the Avalanche jumped out to a 5–0 first-period lead. There were also four fights in the opening 20 minutes, including a bout between Moore and Cooke. Throughout the game the Colorado player was challenged to drop his gloves, but he kept skating away from trouble.

Then, with 8:41 left in the third period, Moore was confronted by minor league call-up Sean Pronger. Moore turned away from Pronger and ignored another challenge from Bertuzzi. The 240-pound Canucks forward gave chase and caught up to Moore at center ice. Suddenly, with his glove still on, Bertuzzi hit Moore in the head with a sucker punch from behind. The Avs forward was knocked unconscious by the right hook and collapsed face-first to the ice; Bertuzzi fell on Moore's back.

Bertuzzi was rushed from the ice with a match penalty. Before other altercations could get going, players from both sides realized Moore's condition was serious and allowed trainers and doctors to get on the ice. The once-angry Vancouver crowd grew silent as a stretcher was called and Moore's head and spine were immobilized. Several minutes later, he was rushed to hospital.

Moore had suffered a severe concussion and three fractured vertebrae in his neck. The incident was replayed on television newscasts and sports highlight shows across North America. The brutal, ugly side of hockey was once again on show for all to see and judge. Both Naslund and May apologized for Bertuzzi's actions and said the team would support their talented star.

The next day Bertuzzi faced the press and, fighting back tears, offered his own apology. "To the fans of hockey and the fans of Vancouver, for the kids that watch this game, I'm truly sorry," he said. "I don't play the game that way. I'm not a mean-spirited person. I'm sorry for what happened."

The NHL immediately suspended the Vancouver forward for the rest of the regular season and the playoffs. The Vancouver Police Department also investigated and, months later, charged Bertuzzi with assault causing bodily harm, a charge that he would later plead guilty to, receiving a conditional discharge with 20 hours of community service. Bertuzzi also lost about $500,000 in salary while suspended by the league. Three years after the incident, doctors still have not cleared Moore to resume his hockey career. A $19.5 million U.S. civil suit filed by Moore against Bertuzzi in February 2006 in Ontario Superior Court is ongoing.

On the ice, the Canucks, perhaps surprisingly considering the Bertuzzi-Moore distraction, managed to finish first in the Northwest Division with 101 points (43-29-10) to end Colorado's nine-year run as division champions. Burke made two moves at the trade deadline in March, adding forwards Geoff Sanderson and Martin Rucinsky to help replace the loss of Bertuzzi. After trying out Rucinsky with Naslund and Morrison, Crawford decided that Cooke would take Bertuzzi's spot on the big line. The abrasive right winger fit right in, helping to open up space for his talented line-mates. Despite scoring only two goals in the 15 games after his return from the Moore hit, Naslund still finished fourth in league scoring with 84 points.

In the playoffs, the Canucks were matched against their old rivals, the Calgary Flames. Despite the loss of Bertuzzi, Vancouver was still favoured to win the series and looked sharp in the 5–3 opening win at GM Place. The Canucks tied a franchise record by scoring four power-play goals in eight chances. Game two was a tight-checking defensive battle that the Canucks gave away with a 50-second lapse; first Flames star Jarome Iginla circled around the net to beat Cloutier, and then Matthew Lombardi broke free to knock in a rebound. Bad luck in the playoffs came back to bite Cloutier in the next game at the Saddledome. The Vancouver goalie stretched awkwardly to stop a rebound and sprained his ankle, forcing him out for the rest of the series. Backup Johan Hedberg came in to stop 19 of 20 shots—Naslund and Cooke scored the goals in a 2–1 victory. Hedberg was back in the net for game four, but the Flames outbattled and outhit the Canucks. Calgary goalie Miikka Kiprusoff had an easy shutout in the 4–0 victory. Crawford changed things up for game five in Vancouver as rookie Alex Auld made his first career playoff start in goal. The Canucks out-played their Albertan opponents, but Kiprusoff stopped 31 of 32 shots in a 2–1 Calgary victory.

Calgary was hoping to put the Canucks away on home ice, but Brendan Morrison had other ideas. The Canucks had jumped out to a 4–0 lead, but the Flames stormed back to tie the score and had all the momentum as the extra session began. As the game went on and with both defences running out of gas, Naslund found Morrison with a pass in the corner. Beating the Calgary defence- man, Morrison went to the net. Cooke tied up the other Flames defender, allowing a clear path to the goal. Morrison made no mistake with a zinger of a shot 42:28 into extra time. It was the longest game in the team's history.

Home ice hadn't been much of an advantage in the series, but the fans at GM Place were optimis- tic that the Morrison goal in game six had changed the momentum. Once the deciding game started, however, Calgary looked like any- thing but a dejected team. Iginla was at his inspi- rational best, scoring both Flames goals as the visiting team nursed a 2–1 lead late into the third period. With time running out, Naslund dashed up the ice with Calgary defenders desperately trying to slow him down. The Canucks captain snapped a wrist shot that Kiprusoff couldn't cleanly handle. Cooke banged in the rebound with only 5.7 seconds remaining, and once again the Vancouver faithful were hoping that the Flames would finally fold. The overtime began with Ed Jovanovski sitting in the penalty box on a slashing call that had carried over from late in the third period. Just 1:25 into the extra session, Iginla fired a shot at Alex Auld. Former Canuck Martin Gelinas pounced on the rebound and, with Auld sprawled out on the ice, lifted a shot into the open net.

For the third time in four years, Vancouver had been eliminated in the first round of the playoffs, and for the second straight year they had lost a seventh game on home ice. It was a bitter disappointment for the fans—this one even more of a "what if..." after the suspension of Bertuzzi. Vancouver had battled the eventual Stanley Cup finalists to overtime in the seventh game without the best power forward in hockey.

Not unexpectedly, Brian Burke was not signed to a new contract. Burke's public declaration in February had embarrassed the Orca Bay brass. Without a deep playoff run, the Irishman had left himself vulnerable. Still, most hockey fans in the city were understandably apprehensive about the decision. Burke had skillfully rebuilt a broken franchise. No one wanted to see the team begin drifting away from the model that had brought respectability back to the Canucks.

Chapter Thirteen

One More Try

Three days after Brian Burke was released, the Canucks announced the hiring of Dave Nonis as the team's ninth general manager. It was a logical in-house promotion; for six seasons he had been responsible for negotiating player contracts and overseeing the team's minor league affiliate in Winnipeg. "Growing up in Vancouver, it was always my dream to one day play for this team," said Nonis when the announcement was made. "It was a dream come true to actually work for the team that you watched growing up. I can tell you, I never imagined having the opportunity to run this team."

The baby-faced Nonis was the team's first general manager who had been born and raised in the Vancouver area. He had played for the Burnaby Bluehawks of the B.C. Junior Hockey League from 1982 to 1984, had left Canada to attend college in the U.S., where he was captain for two years on the University of Maine hockey team, and then played one season of professional hockey in Europe.

Nonis, 37, inherited one of the most talented teams in the NHL, backed by a solid organizational structure that he had helped build under Burke. However, he was left to deal with some of the residual issues left behind from the troubled 2003–04 campaign. First there was the Todd Bertuzzi situation. His suspension had been indefinite, and when the league did reinstate him, Nonis would have to decide if it was in everyone's best interests to have the talented but moody winger remain with the team. The status of Markus Naslund was also uncertain. The captain had only one year left on his contract and had earlier hinted that it might be his last year in the NHL. He had publicly stated that he wanted to raise his children in Sweden.

Naslund was coming off a season where he had suffered a concussion, watched his best friend Bertuzzi self-destruct and seen his team lose another seventh game on home ice. More than any other player, Naslund had been responsible for the on-ice rebirth of the franchise. In his four years as Canucks captain, he had become the best left winger in hockey, averaging 41 goals per season. Naslund had quietly become the face of the team, and his return was crucial to Vancouver remaining a league power.

Within the context of the team's problems was the imminent collision between owners and players as a labour impasse loomed. Gary Bettman and the teams' owners were determined to implement a salary cap, a system the NHL Players' Association vehemently opposed. Both sides dug in for a long fight, and as deadline after deadline passed, the NHL finally announced that the 2004–05 season would be cancelled. For the first time since 1918–19, when a flu epidemic forced the playoffs to be abandoned, there would be no Stanley Cup winner.

With labour strife dominating the hockey headlines, the Canucks made news in November when it was announced that Francesco Aquilini would purchase 50 percent of the team from John McCaw. Aquilini was a local businessman, the managing director of the Aquilini Investment Group, which had real estate holdings across North America. Two years later, Aquilini would buy out the remaining 50 percent of the team from McCaw, putting the team back in the hands of local ownership.

During the summer of 2005, the league and the players finally came together to announce that a settlement had been reached. The owners won the salary cap issue; the cap would be fixed as a percentage of league revenues, making the two sides business partners for the first time. For the 2005–06 campaign, the cap was set at $39 million U.S., a number the Canucks were nudging as the season opened. The league also approved several rule changes: the elimination of the center red line, a reduction in the size of goalie equipment and a shootout after overtime. In order to encourage more offence, referees were also instructed to strictly enforce all stick infractions and obstruction-type penalties. The "new" NHL seemed ideally suited for Vancouver-style hockey.

Nonis decided to keep his team together for 2005–06. Bertuzzi, Ohlund, Jovanovski and Cloutier were all under contract. Over the summer Nonis inked free-agent Naslund to an $18 million, three-year deal, and then Morrison signed for $9.6 million over three years. The Canucks had all the core players under contract—the team Brian Burke had assembled would get one more shot. As the season started, a playoff position was a given; success in the post-season was how the Canucks would be evaluated by their fans.

The first omen as to how the year might unfold came in December. Dan Cloutier was lost to the team with a season-ending knee injury. Alex Auld was elevated as number one goalie and rose to the challenge of playing in net for an offensive-minded team that gave up a lot of scoring chances. Another blow came the same month when the team found out that Ed Jovanovski would miss 38 games with an abdominal injury.

Since coming from Florida in the trade for Bure, "Jovo" had developed into one of the best defencemen in the NHL. A combination of skill, speed and grit had made him a crowd favorite and a leader in the dressing room. The ingredients he brought to the rink each night can be best illustrated by his role in one unforgettable game against Colorado in his first full season in Vancouver. In just over 26 minutes of playing time, Jovanovski scored the winning goal in the third period, threw a game-high seven hits, blocked a game-high four shots, drew two penalties and punched out Avalanche forward Adam Deadmarsh in a fight that changed the momentum of the game. After Vancouver's 4–3 victory, the fans at GM Place didn't rush home as usual. They waited on their feet to give the lanky defenceman a standing ovation when he was announced as the undisputed first star.

Vancouver was still hanging onto a playoff position when the league took a two-week break to allow NHL players to compete in the Olympics at Turin, Italy. In a further turn of bad luck, Ohlund and Salo were injured during the Olympic tournament. Ohlund missed only four games, but was still hampered by his injury when he returned. Salo missed the remainder of the season with a shoulder separation.

The team floundered without its top three defencemen. More disturbing was the increasingly indifferent play of Bertuzzi. He started taking costly penalties and abandoning the defensive responsibilities of his game. He sat at the very end of the bench, isolating himself from Crawford and his teammates. Vancouver fans had remained surprisingly loyal to Bertuzzi through the Steve Moore incident, but they began to show their impatience with his uninterested demeanour.

The Naslund-Morrison-Bertuzzi combination remained Vancouver's top line, but the Sedins, along with line-mate Anson Carter, gradually took over as the team's most consistent offensive force. The twins would dominate entire shifts, cycling the puck in the opponent's zone, looking for Carter to find some space in front of the net for a quick shot. Carter ended up leading the team with a personal-best 33 goals.

As the season reached the stretch run, Vancouver was desperately trying to protect its tenuous playoff position. Nonis added defensive help at the trade deadline, obtaining veterans Eric Weinrich, Keith Carney and Sean Brown for future considerations or draft picks. Fans were hopeful that the return of Jovanovski would rekindle the team's confidence. With the last playoff spot theirs for the taking, the Canucks lost six of their last seven games. In three of the contests, the Canucks were unable to hold leads. For the first time since 2000, the team missed the post-season when Edmonton finished eighth.

The team had never been a cohesive group. Nonis flatly stated that there would be changes to the core of the team. The first casualty was coach Marc Crawford. Despite guiding the Canucks to the playoffs in four of his seven seasons, Crawford's team had managed to win only one post-season series. In changing the makeup of the team, Nonis would be bound by a salary cap of $44 million for the upcoming season. Some tough decisions were being forced upon the rookie general manager to work within the new salary structure.

In June, Vancouver shipped Bertuzzi, Auld and defenceman Bryan Allen to Florida for goalie Roberto Luongo, defenceman Lukas Krajicek and a sixth-round draft pick. It was the biggest trade of the summer—many experts predicted greatness for Luongo, but the 27-year-old had never been in the playoffs or played in the fishbowl of a Canadian market. The move of Bertuzzi to Florida was less surprising. Mike Keenan was the Panthers general manager and, when in Vancouver, had traded to get Bertuzzi from the Islanders in the Linden deal. Keenan was gambling that a change of scenery in a less-intense hockey market would get the power forward back on track. Florida had been willing to trade Luongo because they could not sign him to a long-term deal. Nonis moved quickly to make the all-star netminder the foundation of the team. Within a week of the trade, the Canucks general manager signed Luongo to a four-year deal worth $27 million.

The Luongo signing triggered a change in direction. Securing one of the best goalies in the world meant the Canucks could no longer afford to keep all their offensive talent. Carter was not re-signed, and Jovanovski's stock had risen above the team's budget. The Phoenix Coyotes signed him as a free agent. To fill Jovo's spot, Nonis added stay-at-home defenceman Willie Mitchell. Cloutier was also traded to free up some much needed cap space. The often-injured goalie went to Los Angeles to rejoin new Kings coach Marc Crawford.

Nonis also had a coaching vacancy to fill. No one was surprised when he decided to stay within the organization by promoting Manitoba Moose bench boss Alain Vigneault. A former rough-and-tumble defenceman at the minor league level, "Bam Bam," as he was nicknamed, had moved up the coaching ranks to become head coach for the Montréal Canadiens. In the pressure-cooker of Montréal, Vigneault had managed to get a mediocre Habs team into the Eastern Conference semi-final in his first year behind the bench. His challenge in Vancouver would be much the same: to prod and poke a much less dynamic group of talent into a post-season spot.

Chapter Fourteen

Bobby Lou and Bam Bam

How do you define leadership in sports? There's an aura of intensity—that Mark Messier look of concentration, power and presence that commands attention. And then it has to be backed up by performance—the ability to take over a game when it's on the line. When Roberto Luongo was pictured on the cover of *The Hockey News* during the 2006–07 season, his dark eyes meant business. Within the article he flatly stated, "I will be in the playoffs this year. Nothing will stop me."

It was a bold declaration and one many hockey experts thought would be hard to back up. Dave Nonis had dismantled the team. The run-and-gun Canucks were a memory. To win now, they would have to employ a puck-possession game, backed by strong positional play and almost flawless goaltending. Most pundits picked the team to miss the playoffs in the very competitive Western Conference.

The offence would run through the Sedins. Naslund and Morrison would be the foundation of the second line. Nonis added free-agents Taylor Pyatt, Jan Bulis and Marc Chouinard to provide some secondary scoring. Ohlund, Mitchell and Salo would get the bulk of ice-time on the blue line, with Krajieck, Rory Fitzpatrick, Kevin Bieksa and rookie first-rounder Luc Bourdon competing for the other spots.

The Canucks started the season with a successful road trip and stayed above .500 through the first month. Then reality clicked in as the goals dried up. The Sedins started slowly, Naslund had a 17-game scoring drought and Morrison lost a step after coming back from off-season hip surgery. Of the newcomers, only Pyatt surpassed expectations in his role as the third guy with the Sedins. Vigneault played Bulis with everyone, but he couldn't seem to settle in with any of his line-mates. Chouinard was a bust from the start of the year and by the halfway mark was sent down to Manitoba.

Through the first 35 games, Vancouver's offence was ranked near the bottom of the league. Vigneault kept his sense of humour about his stone-handed group. After eking out a 1–0 win over lowly Columbus, the Canucks coach giggled when asked about a potential two-on-one scoring chance that ended with a Vancouver player putting himself offside. "It's a great game, a lot of fun," said Vigneault. "And I want the guys to relish the competition and come to the rink and give it their best. That's what I try to do." Vigneault brought light-heartedness to the situation, a stark contrast to the tense edginess that Crawford projected when things weren't going well. Even at the most trying of times, Vigneault never showed that he was down on his team.

As the team struggled, the most pleasant surprise was the development of Bieksa. The rugged defenceman with the permanent frown moved up the depth chart as the year progressed. His offensive production was the shocker as he led the Canucks blue liners with 42 points and teamed with Mitchell to face the opposition's top players each night. The rookie, Bourdon, looked overmatched in the nine games he played in the big league and was sent back to junior hockey.

And then there was Luongo. Most Vancouver fans had only seen him play a handful of games, but people in the league who had watched the Montréal native in his days with Florida all agreed he was one of the best goalies in hockey. With all the hype, the Canucks netminder seemed only slightly better than average through the first three months of the season. He wasn't among the top 10 goalies in goals-against average, save percentage or shutouts.

By Christmas, the team had fallen to 17-18-1 and were out of a playoff spot. The turnaround began in a two-game series against the Calgary Flames. On Boxing Day before a boisterous crowd in Vancouver, the Canucks edged the Flames 6–5 in overtime, despite coughing up a pair of two-goal leads. In Calgary two nights later, Vancouver completed the sweep with a gritty 3–2 win.

Those victories provided the spark that Vigneault was hoping his team would find. The Canucks went on a prolonged run; their record from Boxing Day onward was an amazing 32-8-6, collecting 70 out of a possible 92 points. Luongo led the charge. He finished the season playing in 76 of the team's 82 games and claimed a new team record with 47 wins, one off the league record set by Martin Brodeur. Luongo's goals-against average was 2.28, and his save percentage was a sparkling .921. The local media touted "Bobby Lou" as the league MVP. After each amazing save, fans at GM Place would serenade the talented goalie with "Looooou."

As the season turned around, the goals began to trickle in. Never to be confused with an offensive juggernaut, the team's scorers did enough to

win games. The Sedins had breakout seasons—
Daniel led Vancouver with 36 goals and 48
assists, and Henrik shattered Andre Boudrias'
32-year team record of 62 assists with 71 helpers.
As a secondary scorer, Naslund finished with 24
goals and 36 assists. The Vancouver captain could
have made a fuss about his new place on the
team, but he put his personal statistics aside to
play a different role within Vigneault's system.
Morrison found his skating stride and added 20
goals and 31 assists.

As the wins kept mounting, the team amended
its goal of just making the playoffs. On the second last day of the regular season, the Canucks
clinched the Northwest Division title with a victory in San Jose. The team that was most picked
to miss the playoffs finished the season with
a 49-26-7 record. The 49 victories and 105 points
were the best in franchise history. Vancouver led
the league in penalty killing and had the fourth-
best defensive record. At the trade deadline,
Nonis added more depth in two key positions.
Defenceman Brent Sopel returned to Vancouver
in a deal with Los Angeles, and Bryan Smolinski
was obtained from Chicago to replace injured
forward Ryan Kesler. The expectation from
Canucks fans had changed from making the
playoffs to taking a post-season run.

The first obstacle was the Dallas Stars, a team that was almost a mirror image of the Canucks. Dallas relied on a defensive system backed by the goaltending of Marty Turco. After a three-year drought, the playoffs opened in Vancouver with the towels waving at GM Place.

Roberto Luongo's post-season debut was one that will be remembered for a long time. At 18:06 of the fourth overtime period, Henrik Sedin converted a pass from his brother Daniel to end the longest game in franchise history and the sixth-longest ever in the NHL. In the 5–4 win, Luongo stopped 72 of a playoff record 76 shots, 30 of them in overtime. The nail-biting victory came at a high cost. Cooke suffered a groin injury, and Kesler, in his first game back after hip surgery, broke a finger. Both were lost for the rest of the playoffs.

Two nights later the teams were back on the ice, and Dallas was the much fresher team. The Stars rolled to a 2–0 victory over a tired-looking Canucks squad and gained the coveted split on the road. In game three, Dallas dominated the first two periods, but Luongo was superb, holding the home team to a 1–0 lead. Bulis tied the score early in the third period and Vancouver began to take over the game, firing 15 shots at Turco. For the second time in the series, it would take an overtime goal to decide things—this time it took only 7:47 of extra time for Pyatt's one-timer to put the Canucks back on top.

Vancouver pulled away to a 3–1 series lead as Canucks icon Linden's playoff scoring touch returned in game four. In the 2–1 victory, he turned back the clock to look like the Linden of 1994, when he was Vancouver's best player in the Stanley Cup run. On the winning goal, the 37-year-old created a turnover in the Dallas zone and then stormed to the front of the net to slip in a rebound off a Willie Mitchell shot at 14:29 of the third period. Mitchell saved the day a few minutes later when he reached around Luongo to sweep a puck off the goal line to preserve the victory. By taking both games in Dallas, the Canucks had the Stars on the brink of elimination.

Vancouver fans were hoping their team could finish things off at home, but after battling to a scoreless tie in regulation play, Dallas won it when captain Brenden Morrow tipped in a Sergei Zubov point shot at 6:22 of overtime. The Dallas win created some ripples of nervousness in the city—were the Canucks capable of blowing another 3–1 series lead like they did against Minnesota in 2003? Fans were in full panic mode two nights later as the Stars completely dominated Vancouver in a 2–0 victory.

For one of the few times in the season, Vigneault's good humor disappeared. In a short, terse press conference after the game, the Vancouver coach criticized his team's work effort and the play of the veteran players. Turco had posted three shutouts in the series to tie an NHL record. The Sedins and Naslund had been kept off the score sheet since the first game. The Canucks power play had scored only one goal in the series. It seemed the days of November had returned; the team's modest offence had completely disappeared.

The series finale at GM Place was another test of faith when Dallas came out of the first period with a 1–0 lead. Henrik Sedin finally broke Turco's 167:04 shutout streak on the power play to tie the game. At the 7:00 mark of the third period on another Canucks man-advantage, Linden deflected an Ohlund point shot past the Dallas netminder. The game-winner was Linden's 34th playoff goal, tying Pavel Bure's franchise record. Pyatt and Smolinski would add empty-netters in the 4–1 win.

"This win is both one of relief and elation," summed up Brendan Morrison afterward. "We were challenged and our character was questioned. People were asking: Can this core group of guys win a big game? Could they do it?"

Next up was a second-round clash against the big and mean Anaheim Ducks. Anaheim had finished just five points ahead of Vancouver, but the team was a deep squad featuring Chris Pronger and Scott Niedermayer, two of the best defencemen in hockey. The series had an appealing side story: the return of Brian Burke to Vancouver as the general manager of the Ducks. It was Burke against Nonis—mentor versus protegé.

The Ducks were well rested after taking care of Minnesota in five games. Vancouver's grueling seven-game marathon against Dallas had ended with undisclosed injuries to defencemen Salo and Bieksa. The undermanned Canucks were no match for the Ducks in game one. After Jeff Cowan opened the scoring, Anaheim replied with five straight goals in the 5–1 shellacking.

After giving up a pair of power play goals in game one, the theme for the second encounter, from a Vancouver viewpoint, was staying out of the penalty box. In a gritty, if somewhat lucky, game two, a much more disciplined Canucks team eked out a 2–1, double-overtime victory. Linden and Cowan teamed up on the winning goal, with Linden outfighting a Ducks defender in the corner and sending a short pass to Cowan, who somehow slipped a low shot between the post and the pad of goaltender J.S. Giguere. Luongo returned to form with 43 saves.

Cowan had become a crowd favorite in Vancouver since the team claimed him off waivers from Los Angeles in December. At the time, the rugged forward was added to give the team some much-needed abrasiveness. Unexpectedly, Cowan went on a scoring binge in March, scoring seven goals to become an important player down the stretch run leading to the playoffs.

With Salo back in the lineup for game three in Vancouver, a more confident Vancouver team dominated the first period, only to be tied 1–1. The Anaheim goal came off a turnover by Luongo, as the Canucks outshot the Ducks 13–2. Both teams traded goals in the second. At 7:51 of the third period, Corey Perry scored the winner on an Anaheim power play. The Canucks pressured the Ducks in the final few minutes, but Giguere made great saves off Pyatt, Naslund and Daniel Sedin.

Game four was a must-win for Vancouver, but the team received some bad news when Cowan was lost for the post-season with a knee injury. Bieksa, however, made a surprise recovery and suited up. Things started well when Naslund scored the only goal of the first period, and then Morrison made it 2–0 late in the second. Early in the third period, Pronger scored to make the Vancouver crowd a little nervous. The Canucks began to sit back, and the Ducks took advantage. With under six minutes remaining, Teemu Selanne banged in a rebound off a Pronger shot to quiet GM Place. The comeback was completed at 2:07 of overtime when Travis Moen converted a Scott Niedermayer rebound. It was a shocking outcome for a Vancouver side that had managed to battle back from adversity all season.

The Canucks were hoping to survive game five in Anaheim to bring the series back home. Vancouver seemed anything but desperate for the first two periods as the Ducks outshot the visitors 39–13. Luongo made save after save, but couldn't stop Samuel Pahlsson early in the second period after being shoved into his own net. The Canucks came to life in the third and were rewarded when Alex Burrows scored off a Josh Green rebound to send the game into overtime. Luongo kicked out 14 more Anaheim shots in the first extra session. At 4:30 of the second overtime, the Ducks won the series off a bizarre play started by a huge hit from Rob Niedermayer on rookie Jannik Hansen in the Canucks zone. The puck squirted up the boards to brother Scott Niedermayer, who, in one motion, wristed the puck toward the Vancouver net. As the shot was coming through, Luongo had turned toward the referee to complain about the hit. With the goalie's attention diverted, the puck skimmed into the net.

It was a huge gaffe by the all-star netminder, but after being outshot 63–27 in the game and outplayed for most of the series, it was clear that the Ducks were the team that deserved to move on to the next round. The 2006–07 season had marked a major turnaround for the franchise. Dave Nonis had made his mark as the new boss, remaking the team. *The Hockey News* named him Executive of the Year. Vigneault transformed the team's work ethic—over the season, the Canucks built a reputation as one of the hardest groups to play against. The rookie bench boss was later named NHL Coach of the Year.

And Vancouver had a new game breaker. Roberto Luongo surpassed everyone's expectations in his first season as a Canuck. The league acknowledged his astonishing feats when he was named a finalist for the Hart (league MVP), Vezina (top goalie) and Lester B. Pearson (MVP as selected by players) trophies. The Canucks have a new foundation to build from; the next challenge is to find the complementary pieces to make another run for that first Stanley Cup.

The Stats

Legend

GP = Games Played
G = Goals
A = Assists
P = Points
W = Wins

L = Losses
T = Ties
OTL = Overtime Losses
GF = Goals For
GA = Goals Against

Scoring Leaders

Player	GP	G	A	P
Trevor Linden	1081	311	410	721
Markus Naslund	802	321	380	701
Stan Smyl	896	262	411	673
Thomas Gradin	613	197	353	550
Pavel Bure	428	254	224	478
Tony Tanti	531	250	220	470
Todd Bertuzzi	518	199	261	449
Don Lever	583	196	221	407
Andre Boudrias	458	121	267	388
Petri Skriko	472	171	202	373

Regular Season Record in the NHL

Season	GP	W	L	T	OTL	GF	GA	P
1970–71	78	24	46	8	N/A	229	296	56
1971–72	78	20	50	8	N/A	203	297	48
1972–73	78	22	47	9	N/A	233	339	53
1973–74	78	24	43	11	N/A	224	296	59
1974–75	80	38	32	10	N/A	271	254	86
1975–76	80	33	32	15	N/A	271	272	81
1976–77	80	25	42	13	N/A	235	294	63
1977–78	80	20	43	17	N/A	239	320	57
1978–79	80	25	42	13	N/A	217	291	63
1979–80	80	27	37	16	N/A	256	281	70
1980–81	80	28	32	20	N/A	289	301	76
1981–82	80	30	33	17	N/A	290	286	77
1982–83	80	30	35	15	N/A	303	309	75
1983–84	80	32	39	9	N/A	306	328	73
1984–85	80	25	46	9	N/A	282	333	59
1985–86	80	23	44	13	N/A	284	401	59
1986–87	80	29	43	8	N/A	282	314	66
1987–88	80	25	46	9	N/A	272	320	59
1988–89	80	33	39	8	N/A	251	253	74
1989–90	80	25	41	14	N/A	245	306	64
1990–91	80	28	43	9	N/A	243	315	65
1991–92	80	46	26	12	N/A	285	250	96
1992–93	84	46	29	9	N/A	346	278	101
1993–94	84	41	40	3	N/A	279	276	85
1994–95	48	18	18	12	N/A	153	148	48
1995–96	82	32	35	15	N/A	278	278	79
1996–97	82	35	40	7	N/A	257	273	77
1997–98	82	25	43	14	N/A	224	273	64

Regular Season Record in the NHL continued

Season	GP	W	L	T	OTL	GF	GA	P
1998–99	82	23	47	12	N/A	192	258	58
1999–2000	82	30	29	15	8	227	237	83
2000–01	82	36	28	11	7	239	238	90
2001–02	82	42	30	7	3	254	211	94
2002–03	82	45	23	13	1	264	208	104
2003–04	82	43	24	10	5	235	194	101
2004–05	Season cancelled by lockout							
2005–06	82	42	32	N/A	8	256	255	92
2006–07	82	49	26	N/A	7	217	197	105

Regular Season Finish and Playoff Record

Season	Regular Season	Playoffs
1970–71	6th, East Division	Did not qualify
1971–72	7th, East Division	Did not qualify
1972–73	7th, East Division	Did not qualify
1973–74	7th, East Division	Did not qualify
1974–75	1st, Smythe Division	Lost quarter-final
1975–76	2nd, Smythe Division	Lost preliminary round
1976–77	4th, Smythe Division	Did not qualify
1977–78	3rd, Smythe Division	Did not qualify
1978–79	2nd, Smythe Division	Lost preliminary round
1979–80	3rd, Smythe Division	Lost preliminary round
1980–81	3rd, Smythe Division	Lost preliminary round
1981–82	2nd, Smythe Division	Lost Stanley Cup final
1982–83	3rd, Smythe Division	Lost division semi-final
1983–84	3rd, Smythe Division	Lost division semi-final
1984–85	5th, Smythe Division	Did not qualify
1985–86	4th, Smythe Division	Lost division semi-final
1986–87	5th, Smythe Division	Did not qualify
1987–88	5th, Smythe Division	Did not qualify
1988–89	4th, Smythe Division	Lost division semi-final
1989–90	5th, Smythe Division	Did not qualify
1990–91	4th, Smythe Division	Lost division semi-final
1991–92	1st, Smythe Division	Lost division final
1992–93	1st, Smythe Division	Lost division final
1993–94	2nd, Pacific Division	Lost Stanley Cup final
1994–95	2nd, Pacific Division	Lost conference semi-final
1995–96	3rd, Pacific Division	Lost conference quarter-final
1996–97	4th, Pacific Division	Did not qualify
1997–98	7th, Pacific Division	Did not qualify

Regular Season Finish and Playoff Record continued

Season	Regular Season	Playoffs
1998–99	4th, Northwest Division	Did not qualify
1999–2000	3rd, Northwest Division	Did not qualify
2000–01	3rd, Northwest Division	Lost conference quarter-final
2001–02	2nd, Northwest Division	Lost conference quarter-final
2002–03	2nd, Northwest Division	Lost conference semi-final
2003–04	1st, Northwest Division	Lost conference quarter-final
2004–05	Season cancelled by lockout	
2005–06	4th, Northwest Division	Did not qualify
2006–07	1st, Northwest Division	Lost conference semi-final

Notes on Sources

Banks, Kerry. *The Riddle of the Russian Rocket*. Vancouver: Greystone Books, 2001.

Boyd, Denny. *History of Hockey in BC: From the Denman Arena to the Pacific Coliseum*. Vancouver: Canucks Publishing Ltd., 1970.

Boyd, Denny. *The Vancouver Canucks Story*. Vancouver: Canucks Publishing Ltd., 1973.

Farris, Jason, et al. *Hockey Play-By-Play: Around the NHL with Jim Robson*. Vancouver: CircaNow Productions, 2005.

Gallagher, Tony, et al. *Towels, Triumph and Tears: The Vancouver Canucks and their Amazing Drive to the 1982 Stanley Cup Final*. Madiera Park: Harbour Publishing, 1982.

Imlach, Punch, et al. *Heaven and Hell in the NHL*. Toronto: McClelland and Stewart Limited, 1982.

Jewison, Norm. *The Vancouver Canucks: The First Twenty Years*. Winlaw: Polestar Press, 1990.

Rossiter, Sean. *Vancouver Canucks: The Silver Edition*. Vancouver: Opus Productions Inc., 1994.

Whitehead, Eric. *The Patricks: Hockey's Royal Family*. Toronto: Doubleday Canada Limited, 1980.

Vancouver Canucks (Hockey Team). *Vancouver Canucks Official Yearbook.* Vancouver: Canucks Publishing Ltd., 1970–2006.

Web Sources

Vancouver Canucks (n.d.) www.canucks.com. Retrieved March 1 to May 12, 2007.

Information was also used from the following print outlets:

Alberni Valley Times, Calgary Herald, Cape Breton Post, Daily News (Prince Rupert), *Edmonton Journal, Kingston Whig-Standard, Nanaimo Daily News, National Post, Vancouver Province, Vancouver Sun.*

Stephen Drake

Stephen Drake was born in Vancouver and grew up on a ranch near Merritt, BC. He learned to play hockey by skating for hours each weekend with his friends on Nicola Lake. He also enrolled in hockey schools, has played with the same group of friends for 15 years and was a member of the infamous DOA punk rock hockey team when they trounced a local radio station's all-star squad. His hockey group also rented the Pacific Coliseum for one game, and Stephen got to skate on the same ice surface as his beloved Canucks. These days he's a freelance writer living in New Westminster with his wife and two young children.

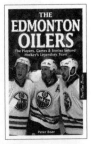
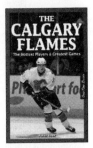
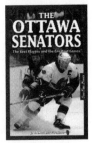